Vintage Bedspreads to Crochet

31 Vintage Bedspread Patterns to Crochet - A Collection of Vintage Bedspreads Crochet Patterns

Craftdrawer Crafts

ISBN # 978-1797578316

Crochet Vintage Bedspreads – A collections of 31 vintage bedspread patterns. These lovely vintage patterns feature a variety of different designs and textures. Patterns for twin size and full-size beds. Can be adusted to Queen and King size.

31 Vintage Bedspread Patterns to Crochet

Compiled by Bookdrawer – Craftdrawer Crafts

Craftdrawer Copyright © 2019 All Rights Reserved

Patterns may not be reproduced, sold in any format except for you may print copies for personal use in order to crochet the patterns.

Note: Materials used in these patterns are from an original vintage patterns - Yarns and needles will have to be changed or updated by the reader.

Copyright © Craftdrawer Crafts All Rights Reserved

Contents

Introduction	5
Crochet Abbrevations	6
Crochet Vintage Bedspread Patterns	7
Crochet Petal Bedspread	7
Rose Bedspread	11
Irish Crochet Bedspread	14
Popcorn Stitches Bedspread	16
Popcorn Bedspread	19
Pineapple Bedspread	21
The Petite Bedspread	23
California Bedspread	27
Filet Block Bedspread	30
Italian Rose Bedspread	33
Grandma's Garden Bedspread	35
Pineapple Pinwheel Bedspread	37
Popcorn Star Bedspread	40
Star Popcorn Bedspread	43
Beauty Rose Bedspread	47
Galaxy Bedspread	50
Popcorn Star Bedspread 2	52
Pineapple Frosting Bedspread	55
Heavenly Daydream Bedspread	60

Royal Society Filet Bedspread	62
The Puritan Bedspread	65
Irish Crochet Bedspread 2	68
Popcorn Bedspread 2	70
Texas Bedspread	73
Wakefield Bedspread	76
Bedspread of Filet	79
Stafford Bedspread	82
Vine Square Bedspread and Pillow	85
Vespers Bedspread	87
Cross Roads Bedspread	90
Royal Irish Rose Bedspread	94
Crochet Notes	97

Introduction

Vintage bedspreads are a timeless way to create something beautiful for a bedroom. Using crochet cotton or thread you can make a lacy bedspread that will become an heirloom for years to come.

A unique collection of vintage bedspreads to crochet. 31 patterns in all, featuring complete instructions and photos of each pattern. These lovely vintage patterns feature a variety of different designs and textures. Patterns for twin size and full-size beds. Instructions can be increased for larger bed sizes.

Since these are vintage patterns the materials that they are crocheted with are updated with suggested yarn, thread or cotton. Use your judgement and crochet skills to modify any pattern to fit the bed that you are making the item for.

The vintage bedspreads range from Irish crochet, filet, popcorn, garden, florals, stars and many more. Patterns can be made for baby, a small bed, large bed, or to add as decoration to a sofa or chair.

With the variety of colors available today in crochet thread and crochet cotton you can easily make these patterns in any color, size or style that you choose.

There are 31 crochet patterns in all to make in Vintage Bedspreads to crochet. You'll be able to crochet a selection of patterns for each room in your home, for gifts, or make something special for decorating the home.

Note: The ability to read crochet patterns and crochet experience required for these detailed patterns.

Notes…….

Abbreviations

ch chain
sp space
sc single crochet
st(s) stitch(es)
half dc half double crochet
rnd round
dc double crochet
incl inclusive
sl st slip stitch
inc increase
dec decrease

dtr double treble (triple) crochet - Yarn over hook three times, then insert hook into next stitch.
Yarn over hook and draw yarn through stitch - five loops on the hook.
Loop yarn over hook and draw through two loops, (there are now four loops remaining on the hook), *yarn over hook and draw through two loops**, repeat * to ** twice more. This completes one double treble crochet.

pc popcorn stitch - The popcorn stitch can be created with a varying number of stitches in the work. Follow the instructions for the number of stitches used in your pattern. To work the popcorn stitch in this version, yarn over, insert hook in stitch, yarn over, pull through stitch, yarn over, pull through 2 lps twice. Do this 5 times so there are 5 stitches in the popcorn stitch, drop loop from hook, insert hook from front to back through top of first stitch made, pull dropped loop through stitch, yarn over, pull through loop.

* (asterisk) . . . Repeat the instructions following the asterisk as many times as specified.

Repeat instructions in parentheses as many times as specified. For example: "**(Ch 5, sc in next sc) 5 times**" means to make all that is in parentheses 5 times in all.

Crochet Vintage Bedspreads Patterns

Petal Bedspread

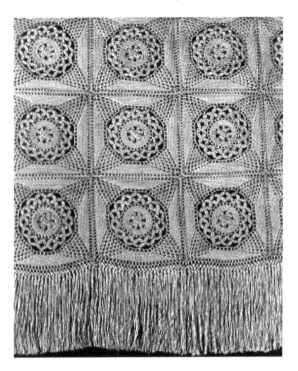

Crochet Petal Bedspread – Original vintage pattern

Double Bedspread - Approx. 84 x 104 inches

For a full-size bedspread make 180 squares, 15 in length and 12 in width.

Original Vintage Materials: 25 Balls or Skeins Knitting and Crochet Cotton, White or Natural.

Suggested Materials - Crochet Thread Size 10 or Use a Crochet Cotton if Preferred for a heavier bedspread

Boye Steel Crochet Hook, No. H/8

Each square will measure about 6¼ inches.

CROCHET SQUARE

Ch 5, join with slip St to form ring.

1st round: Ch 3, 15 DC over ring, join with slip st in 3rd st of ch 3 (16 DC counting beginning ch 3).

2nd round: Ch 5, thread twice over hook, draw up a loop in joining st below, thread over and through 2 loops, twice in succession, retaining the 2 last loops on hook, thread twice over hook, draw up a 2nd loop in same place, over and through 2 loops twice in succession, over and through remaining 3 loops on hook (a petal at beginning of round), ch 6, thread twice over hook, draw up a loop in the same place, over and through 2 loops twice in succession, retaining the last 2 loops on hook, thread twice over hook, draw up a 2nd loop in same place, over and through 2 loops twice in succession, thread twice over hook, draw up a 3rd loop in same place, over and through 2 loops twice in succession, over and through remaining 4 loops on hook (a regular petal), * ch 6, skip 3 DC, work a regular petal in next DC, ch 6, another petal in same st, repeat from * twice, ch 6, join with a slip st in top of first petal.

3rd round: 1 SC in joining st, 6 SC in first ch 6 space, * 1 SC in top of next petal, 6 SC in next ch 6 space, repeat from * 6 times, join with slip st in 1st SC (56 SC).

4th, 5th and 6th rounds: 1 SC in each SC of previous round, working through back loop only of each st, join with slip st in 1st SC of 6th round.

7th round: Ch 5, skip 1 SC, 1 DC in the next SC, * ch 2, skip 1 SC, 1 DC in the next SC, repeat from * 25 times, ch 2, join with slip st in 3rd st of beginning ch 5 (28 spaces).

8th round: 1 SC in 1st space, ch 5, thread twice over hook, draw up a loop in SC just made, thread over and through 2 loops twice in succession (2 loops left on hook), thread twice over hook, draw up a 2nd loop in same st, over and through 2 loops twice in succession, over and through remaining 3 loops on hook (single petal), ch 6, thread twice over hook, draw up a loop in first st of ch 6, thread over and through 2 loops twice in succession, thread twice over hook, draw up a 2nd loop in same st, over and through 2 loops twice in succession, over and through remaining 3 loops, skip 1 space, 1 SC in the next space (this completes double petal), work 13 more double petals, skipping 1 space between petals, join with slip st in 1st SC at beginning of round.

9th round: Slip st to tip of 1st single petal, 1 SC over center of 1st double petal, work a double petal in same manner as on previous row, * 1 SC over center of next double petal, work second double petal, repeat from * 12 times, join with slip st in 1st SC at beginning of round (14 double petals).

10th round: Slip St to tip of 1st single petal, 1 SC over center of 1st double petal of previous row, ch 11, * 1 SC over center of next double petal, ch 11, repeat from * 12 times, join with slip st in 1st SC (14 spaces).

11th round: Ch 5, * 1 DC in 3rd st of ch 11, ch 2, skip 2 sts, 1 DC in next st, ch 2, skip 2 sts, 1 DC in next st, ch 2, skip 2 sts, 1 DC in SC, ch 2, skip 2 sts, repeat from * 13 times, join with slip st in 3rd st of beginning ch 5 (56 spaces).

12th round: 2 SC in 1st space, * 1 SC in DC, 2 SC in next space, repeat from * 5 times (20 SC), ch 2, 2 DC in each of next 7 spaces, with ch 2 between blocks, **ch 2, 2 SC in each of next 7 spaces, with 1 SC in each DC between spaces, ch 2, 2 DC in each of next 7 spaces, with ch 2 between blocks, repeat from ** twice, ch 2, join with slip st to 1st SC.

13th round: Working through back loop only, 1 SC in each SC, 1 SC in each st of 1st ch-2, ch 2, 2 DC in each of next 6 spaces, with ch 2 between blocks, ch 2, * 1 SC in each st of next ch-2, 1 SC in each of next 20 SC, 1 SC in each st of next ch-2 (24 SC), ch 2, 2 DC in each of next 6 spaces with ch-2 between blocks, ch 2, repeat from * twice, 1 SC in each St of last ch-2.

14th-18th rounds incl: Work in same manner as 13th round, working 4 more SC and 1 less group of DC in each section, join with slip st in 1st SC.

19th round: Ch 5, skip 1 SC, 1 DC in next st, * ch 2, skip 1 SC, 1 DC in next st, repeat from * to corner, ch 2, 1 DC in space, ch 2, 1 DC between DCs in corner, ch 2, 1 DC in next space, continue in same manner around entire square, join with slip st in 3rd st of ch 5 and fasten off.

For a full-size bedspread make 180 squares, 15 in length and 12 in width.

JOINING

Sew together on wrong side, sewing through back threads of edge stitches and using same thread as for crocheting.

Work one row of meshes around the entire spread as follows: starting in corner DC, ch 5 (to count as 1 DC and ch 2), 1 more DC in same (corner) DC, ch 2, 1 DC in 1st space after corner, ch 2, * 1 DC in next space, ch 2, repeat from * around, working 2 DC with ch 2 between DCs in each corner and 1 DC in each joining between squares, join with slip st in 3rd st of 5 and fasten off.

Fringe

Wind thread around an 8-inch piece cardboard; cut one end. Tie 5 strands in each space. Take 5 strands from one fringe and 5 strands from next fringe and tie together ¾ inch below first knot. Trim edges evenly.

Rose Bedspread

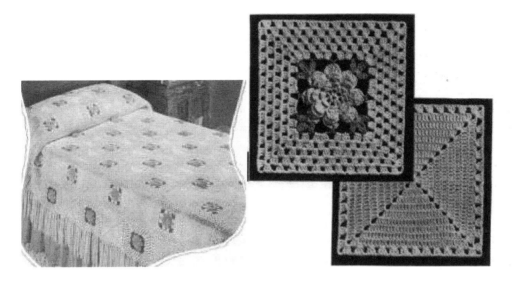

Rose Bedspread – Original Vintage Pattern

Original Materials used - Mercerized Bedspread Cotton:

Single Size Spread, 66 x 108 inches:

35 balls of No. 1 White, 10 balls of No. 46-A Mid Rose and 2 balls of No. 48 Hunter's Green.

Double Size Spread, 78 x 108 inches:

42 balls of No. 1 White, 12 balls of No. 46-A Mid Rose and 3 balls of No. 48 Hunter's Green.

Suggested Materials - Crochet Thread Size 10 or Use a Crochet Cotton if Preferred for a heavier bedspread

Crochet Hook No. 7 (4.5mm)

For a Single Size Spread, make 77 Flower Motifs and 76 Plain Motifs.

For Double Size Spread make 94 Flower Motifs and 93 Plain Motifs.

FLOWER MOTIF . . . Starting at center with Mid Rose, ch 6. Join with sl st to form ring.

1st rnd: Ch 5, (dc in ring, ch 2) 7 times. Join to 3rd ch of ch-5 (8 sps).

2nd rnd: In each sp around make sc, half dc, 3 dc, half dc and sc. Join.

3rd rnd: * Ch 4, sc between next 2 petals. Repeat from * around. Join.

4th rnd: In each loop around make sc, half dc, 5 dc, half dc and sc. Join.

5th rnd: Repeat 3rd rnd.

6th rnd: In each loop around make sc, half dc, 7 dc, half dc and sc. Join.

7th rnd: Repeat 3rd rnd.

8th rnd: In each loop around make sc, half dc, dc, 7 tr, dc, half dc and sc. Join and fasten off.

9th rnd: Attach Hunter Green to center tr of any petal, sc in same place, * ch 7, holding back on hook the last loop of each tr make 3 tr in center tr of next petal, thread over and draw through all loops on hook (cluster made), ch 4, in same tr make 3-d tr cluster, ch 4 and 3-tr cluster; ch 7, sc in center tr of next petal. Repeat from * around. Join and break off.

10th rnd: Attach White to any 3-d tr cluster, ch 3, 2 dc in same place, * ch 1, 3 dc in next sp, (ch 1, in next sp make 3 dc, ch 1 and 3 dc) twice; ch 1, 3 dc in next sp, ch 1, in tip of next cluster make 3 dc, ch 3 and 3 dc. Repeat from * around, ending with 3 dc in same place as first 2 dc, ch 1, dc in top of ch-3.

11th to 14th rnds incl: Ch 3, 2 dc in sp just formed, * ch 1, 3 dc in next sp. Repeat from * around, making 3 dc, ch 3 and 3 dc in ch-3 sp at each corner. Join as before. Break off at end of 14th rnd.

PLAIN MOTIF . . . Starting at center with White, ch 5. Join with sl st to form ring.

1st rnd: Ch 3, 2 dc in ring, (ch 3, 3 dc in ring) 3 times; ch 1, half dc in top of starting chain.

2nd rnd: Ch 3, dc in sp just formed, * dc in next 3 dc, in next sp make 2 dc, ch 3 and 2 dc. Repeat from * around, ending with 2 dc in same place as first dc, ch 1, half dc in top of starting chain.

3rd to 9th rnds incl: Ch 3, dc in sp just formed, * dc in each dc across to corner, in corner sp make 2 dc, ch 3 and 2 dc. Repeat from * around. Join as before.

10th rnd: Ch 3, 2 dc in sp just formed, * (ch 1, skip 3 dc, make 3 dc in next dc) twice; (ch 1, skip 2 dc, make 3 dc in next dc) 8 times; ch 1, in corner sp make 3 dc, ch 3 and 3 dc. Repeat from * around, ending with 3 dc in same place as first 2 dc, ch 3. Join and break off.

For a Single Size Spread, make 77 Flower Motifs and 76 Plain Motifs.

For Double Size Spread make 94 Flower Motifs and 93 Plain Motifs.

Sew Motifs neatly together, alternating Flower and Plain Motifs and making 9 rows of

17 Motifs for Single Size Spread, and 11 rows of 17 Motifs for Double Size Spread.

FRINGE. .... Cut 10 strands of White, each 12 inches long. Double these strands to form a loop. Insert hook in first sp on one long side of Bedspread and draw loop through. Draw loose ends through loop and pull up tightly to form a knot. Make a Fringe in each sp around two long sides and one short side. Trim ends evenly.

Irish Crochet Bedspread

Irish Crochet Bedspread – Original Vintage Pattern

Vintage Materials Used: Mercerized Bedspread Cotton in White or Ecru. Single Size: 35 balls.

Double Size: 43 balls.

Steel Crochet Hook No. H8.

Suggested Materials - Crochet Thread Size 10 or 12 – Optional - Use a Crochet Cotton if Preferred for a heavier bedspread

GAUGE: Each block measures about 6 inches square.

For single size spread about 70 x 106 inches, including fringe, make 11 x 17 blocks.

For double size spread about 88 x 106 inches, including fringe, make 14 x 17 blocks.

BLOCK . . . Ch 8. Join with sl st to form ring.

1st rnd: Ch 1, 16 sc in ring. Join with sl st in 1st sc.

2nd rnd: Ch 1, sc in same place as sl st, * ch 3, skip 1 sc, sc in next sc. Repeat from * around, joining last ch-3 with sl st in 1st sc.

3rd rnd: Sl st in next sp, in each sp around make sc, h dc, 3 dc, h dc and sc (8 petals).

4th rnd: * Ch 5, sc behind next sc on last loop rnd. Repeat from * around, ending with ch 5.

5th rnd: In each loop around make sc, h dc, dc, 4 tr, dc, h dc and sc.

6th rnd: * Ch 6, sc behind next sc on last loop rnd, ch 9, sl st in 9th ch from hook, in this ch-9 loop make sc, h dc, 3 dc, 5 tr, 3 dc, h dc and sc, sl st in sc at base of loop. Repeat from * around.

7th rnd: In each ch-6 loop make sc, h dc, dc, 5 tr, dc, h dc, and sc. Join with sl st in 1st sc of 1st petal.

8th rnd: Sl st in h dc and in dc, ch 1, sc in same place as last sl st, * ch 4, sc in next st, ch 6, skip 3 tr, sc in next st, ch 4, sc in next st, ch 6, sc in dc of next petal. Repeat from * around, joining last ch-6 with sl st in 1st sc.

9th rnd: Sl st in 4 ch, in sc and in next ch, sc in ch-6 loop, ch 4, sc in same loop, * ch 6, in next ch-6 loop make sc, ch 4 and sc. Repeat from * around. Join.

10th rnd: Sl st in 4 ch, in sc and in next 2 ch, ch 4, in same loop make 2 tr, ch 5 and 3 tr, * (ch 6, in next loop make sc, ch 4 and sc) 3 times; ch 6, in next loop make 3 tr, ch 5 and 3 tr. Repeat from * around. Join with sl st in top st of 1st ch-4.

11th rnd: Ch 4, tr in next 2 tr, * in corner sp make 3 tr, ch 5 and 3 tr, tr in next 3 tr, ch 6, sc in next loop, (ch 6, in next loop make sc, ch 4 and sc) twice; ch 6, sc in next loop, ch 6, tr in next 3 tr. Repeat from * around. Join.

12th rnd: Ch 4, tr in 5 tr, * in next loop make 3 tr, ch 5 and 3 tr, tr in 6 tr, 3 tr in next loop, ch 6, sc in next loop, ch 6, in next loop make sc, ch 4 and sc, ch 6, sc in next loop, ch 6, 3 tr in next loop, tr in next 6 tr. Repeat from * around. Join.

13th rnd: Ch 4, tr in 8 tr, * in next loop make 3 tr, ch 5 and 3 tr, tr in 12 tr, 3 tr in next loop, (ch 3, tr in next loop) twice; ch 3, 3 tr in next loop, tr in next 12 tr. Repeat from * around. Join and fasten off.

Make necessary number of blocks and sew them together on wrong side with neat over and-over stitches, catching only one loop of each st on each edge. Attach thread to center st of a corner loop, ch 9, tr in same st, * ch 4, skip 3 sts, tr in next st. Repeat from * around one short and two long edges, making tr, ch 5 and tr at corners. Fasten off.

FRINGE . . . Make fringe in every other sp around one short and two long edges as follows: Cut 25 strands each 9 inches long. Double these strands, forming a loop. Pull loop through 1st sp and draw loose ends through loop. Pull tight. Trim evenly.

Popcorn Stitches Bedspread

Popcorn Stitches Bedspread – Original Vintage Crochet Patterns

Original Materials – Bedspread Cotton

Suggested Materials - Crochet Thread Size 10 or 12 – Optional - Use a Crochet Cotton if Preferred for a heavier bedspread

Single Size Spread - 72 x 108 inches, including fringe 60 balls of White or Ecru, or 86 balls of any color

Double Size Spread - 90 x 108 inches, including fringe 76 balls of White or Ecru, or 109 balls of any color

Steel Crochet Hook No. 7.

GAUGE: Block measures 6 1/2 inches from side to side.

BLOCK . . . Starting at center, ch 12. Join with sl st.

1st rnd: Ch 3, 29 dc in ring. Sl st in top of ch-3.

2nd rnd: Ch 3, * (5 dc in next dc, drop loop from hook, insert hook in 1st dc and draw dropped loop through - pc st made - dc in next dc) twice; ch 2, dc in next dc. Repeat from * around. Sl st in top of ch-3.

3rd rnd: Ch 3, * (pc st in tip of pc st, dc in next dc) twice; ch 4, dc in next dc. Repeat from * around. Join.

4th rnd: Ch 3, * (pc st in next pc st, dc in next dc) twice; ch 6, dc in next dc. Repeat from * around. Join.

5th rnd: Ch 3, pc st in same place as sl st, * (dc in next pc st, pc st in next dc) twice; dc in same place as last pc st, ch 6, in next dc make dc and pc st. Repeat from * around. Join.

6th rnd: Ch 3, 2 dc in same place as sl st, * pc st in same place, (dc in next pc st, pc st in next dc) 3 times; 3 dc in same place as last pc st, ch 4, 3 dc in next dc. Repeat from * around. Join.

7th rnd: Ch 3, pc st in same place as sl st, * dc in next dc, pc st in next dc, dc in next pc st, ch 2, skip next dc and the following pc st, in next dc make 2 dc, ch 3 and 2 dc; ch 2, skip next pc st and the following dc, dc in next pc st, pc st in next dc, dc in next dc, in next dc make pc st and dc; ch 2, in next dc make dc and pc st. Repeat from * around. Join.

8th rnd: Ch 3, make dc and pc st in same place as sl st, * dc in next pc st, pc st in next dc, dc in next pc st, ch 2, dc in next sp, ch 2, in next sp make 2 dc, ch 3 and 2 dc; ch 2, dc in next sp, ch 2, skip next dc, (dc in next pc st, pc st in next dc) twice; 2 dc in same place as last pc st; in next dc make 2 dc and pc st. Repeat from * around. Join.

9th rnd: Ch 3, * (pc st in next dc, dc in next pc st) twice; (ch 2, dc in next sp) twice; ch 2, in next sp make 2 dc, ch 3 and 2 dc; (ch 2, dc in next sp) twice; ch 2, skip 1 dc, (dc in next pc st, pc st in next dc) twice; dc in next dc. Repeat from * around. Join to tip of pc st.

10th rnd: Ch 3, pc st in next dc, dc in next pc st, * (ch 2, dc in next sp) 3 times; dc in next 2 dc, in next sp make 2 dc, ch 3 and 2 dc: dc in next 2 dc, dc in next sp, (ch 2, dc in next sp) twice; ch 2, skip next dc, (dc in next pc st, pc st in next dc) 3 times; dc in next pc st. Repeat from * around. Join.

11th rnd: Sl st in next pc st, ch 5 (to count as dc and ch 2), (dc in next sp, ch 2) twice: * dc in next sp, dc in next 5 dc, in next sp make 2 dc, ch 3 and 2 dc; dc in next 5 dc, dc in next sp, (ch 2, dc in next sp) twice; ch 2, skip next dc, (dc in next pc st, pc st in next dc) twice; dc in next pc st, (ch 2, dc in next sp) twice; ch 2. Repeat from * around. Join and break off.

For Single Size Spread, make 6 rows of 14 Blocks and 5 rows of 15 Blocks.

For Double Size Spread, make 8 rows of 14 Blocks and 7 rows of 15 Blocks.

Sew Blocks neatly together on wrong side, alternating rows of 14 and 15 Blocks (see diagram).

FRINGE . . . Cut 8 lengths of thread each 16 inches long. Double the strands to form a loop. Insert hook in space and draw loop through. Draw loose ends through loop and pull up tightly. Make a fringe in each space around all four sides of spread and trim evenly.

Diagram

Popcorn Bedspread

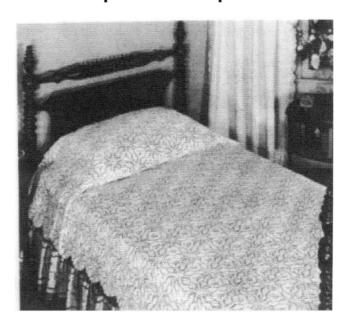

Popcorn Bedspread – Vintage Crochet Pattern

Vintage Materials: Crochet Thread: 80 balls for Single Size; 98 balls for Double Size

Suggested Materials - Crochet Thread Size 10 or 12 – Optional - Use a Crochet Cotton if Preferred for a heavier bedspread

Steel Crochet Hook No. 7 or 8.

Motif measures about 5 1/2 inches from point to opposite point, and about 5 inches from side to opposite side before blocking.

For single size spread about 72 x 105 inches, make 348 motifs; for double size spread about 90 x 105 inches, make 430 motifs.

MOTIF . . Ch 10. Join with sl st.

1st rnd: Ch 3 (to count as dc), 23 dc in ring. Join with sl st in top st of ch-3.

2nd rnd: Ch 4 (to count as dc and ch 1), * dc in next dc, ch 1. Repeat from * around. Join with sl st to 3rd st of ch-4.

3rd rnd: Sl st in next sp, ch 3 to count as dc, in same sp make 2 dc, ch 3 and 3 dc (shell made); * ch 2, skip 1 sp, dc in next sp, ch 2, skip 1 sp, in next sp make 3 dc, ch 3 and 3 dc (another shell made). Repeat from * around. Join.

4th rnd: Sl st in next 2 sts, sl st in next sp, ch 3, complete a shell in same sp; * (ch 2, dc in next sp) twice; ch 2, shell in sp of next shell. Repeat from * around. Join.

5th rnd: Sl st in next 2 sts, sl st in next sp, ch 3, shell in same sp; * ch 2, dc in next sp, ch 2, make a pc st in next sp - to make a pc st, ch 1, 5 dc in next sp, drop loop from hook, insert hook in ch-1 preceding 1st dc of this group and pull dropped loop through-; ch 2, dc in next sp, ch 2, shell in sp of next shell. Repeat from * around. Join.

6th rnd: Sl st in next 2 sts, sl st in next sp, ch 3, shell in same sp; * ch 2, dc in next sp, (ch 2, pc st in next sp) twice; ch 2, dc in next sp, ch 2, shell in sp of next shell. Repeat from * around. Join.

7th rnd: Sl st in next dc, ch 3, pc st in top of next dc, in next sp make dc, ch 3 and dc; pc st in top of next dc, dc in next dc, * ch 2, dc in next sp, ch 2, (pc st in next sp, ch 2) 3 times; dc in next sp, ch 2, skip 1 dc, dc in next dc, pc st in top of next dc, in next sp make dc, ch 3 and dc; pc st in top of next dc, dc in next dc. Repeat from * around. Join.

8th rnd: Ch 3, pc st in same place as sl st, dc in top of pc st, dc in next dc, in next sp make dc, ch 3 and dc; dc in next dc, dc in top of pc st, pc st in top of next dc, * (dc in next sp, ch 2) twice; (pc st in next sp, ch 2) twice; dc in next sp, ch 2, dc in next sp, pc st in top of next dc, dc in top of pc st, dc in next dc, in next sp make dc, ch 3 and dc; dc in next dc, dc in top of next pc st, pc st in top of next dc. Repeat from * around, ending with dc in last sp. Join.

9th rnd: Ch 3, dc in top of pc st, dc in next 3 dc, in next sp make dc, ch 3 and dc; dc in next 3 dc, dc in top of pc st, pc st in next dc, * (dc in next sp, ch 2) twice; pc st in next sp, (ch 2, dc in next sp) twice; pc st in next dc, dc in top of next pc st, dc in next 3 dc, in next sp make dc, ch 3 and dc; dc in next 3 dc, dc in top of next pc st, pc st in next dc. Repeat from * around, ending with dc in last sp, pc st in last dc. Join and break off.

Make necessary number of motifs and sew together on wrong side with neat over-and-over sts, joining them as in diagram for joining hexagon motifs.

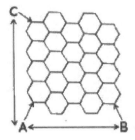

For single size spread make 17 motifs from A to B and 20 motifs from A to C;

For double size spread make 21 motifs from A to B and 20 motifs from A to C.

Pineapple Bedspread

Pineapple Bedspread – The Spool Cotton Company 1946

Vintage Materials: Mercerized Crochet Size 20;

Big Ball: 47 balls for Single Size; 60 balls for Double Size

Suggested Materials - Crochet Thread Size 10 or 12 or 20 – Optional - Use a Crochet Cotton if Preferred for a heavier bedspread

Steel Crochet Hook No. 8 or 9.

Motif measures 4 3/4 inches in diameter before blocking.

For a single size spread about 71 x 104 inches, make 15 x 22 motifs.

For a double size spread about 90 x 104 inches, make 19 x 22 motifs.

FIRST MOTIF . . . Starting at center ch 10. Join with sl st.

1st rnd: Ch 3, dc in ring, (ch 3, 2 dc in ring) 7 times; ch 3, sl st in 3rd st of ch-3.

2nd rnd: Ch 3, dc in next dc, (ch 5, dc in next 2 dc) 7 times; ch 5. Join.

3rd rnd: Ch 3, dc in next dc, * in next sp make 3 dc, ch 2 and 3 dc; dc in next 2 dc. Repeat from * around. Join.

4th rnd: Ch 3, dc in next 2 dc, * in next sp make 2 dc, ch 5 and 2 dc; skip 2 dc, dc in next 4 dc. Repeat from * around. Join.

5th rnd: Ch 3, dc in next 2 dc, * ch 3, 6 tr in next sp, ch 3, skip 2 dc, dc in next 4 dc. Repeat from * around. Join.

6th rnd: Ch 3, dc in next 2 dc, * ch 4, (dc in next tr, ch 2) 5 times; dc in next tr, ch 4, dc in next 4 dc. Repeat from * around. Join.

7th rnd: Ch 3, dc in next 2 dc, * ch 5, skip next sp, sc in next sp, (ch 3, sc in next sp) 4 times; ch 5, skip next sp, dc in next 4 dc. Repeat from * around. Join.

8th rnd: Ch 3, dc in next 2 dc, * ch 6, sc in next ch-3 loop, (ch 3, sc in next loop) 3 times; ch 6, dc in next 4 dc. Repeat from * around. Join.

9th rnd: Ch 3, dc in next 2 dc, 2 dc in next sp, * ch 6, sc in next loop, (ch 3, sc in next loop) twice; ch 6, 2 dc in sp, dc in next 4 dc, 2 dc in next sp. Repeat from * around. Join.

10th rnd: Sl st in next 3 dc, ch 3, dc in next dc, 2 dc in next sp, * ch 6, sc in next loop, ch 3, sc in next loop, ch 6, 2 dc in next sp, dc in next 2 dc, ch 4, skip 4 dc, dc in next 2 dc, 2 dc in next sp. Repeat from * around. Join.

11th rnd: Sl st in next 2 dc, ch 3, dc in next dc, 2 dc in next sp, * ch 6, sc in next loop, ch 6, 2 dc in next sp, dc in next 2 dc, ch 6, sc in next sp, ch 6, skip 2 dc, dc in next 2 dc, 2 dc in next sp. Repeat from * around. Join and break off.

SECOND MOTIF . . . Work as for First Motif until 10th rnd is complete.

11th rnd: Sl st in next 2 dc, ch 3, dc in next dc, 2 dc in next sp, ch 6, sc in next loop, ch 6, 2 dc in next sp, dc in next 2 dc, ch 3, sl st in corresponding sp on First Motif, ch 3, sc in next sp on Second Motif, ch 3, sc in corresponding sp on First Motif, ch 3, dc in next 2 dc on Second Motif, 2 dc in next sp and complete rnd as for First Motif (no more joinings).

Make necessary number of motifs, joining adjacent sides as Second Motif was joined to First Motif, leaving 6 sps free between joinings.

FILL-IN-MOTIF . . . Work first 2 rnds as for First Motif.

3rd rnd: Ch 3, dc in next dc, * dc in next sp, ch 5, dc in same sp, dc in next 2 dc. Repeat from * around. Join.

4th rnd: Ch 3, dc in next 2 dc, ch 3, sl st in 3rd free sp from joining of motifs, * ch 3, sc in next sp on Fill-in-motif, ch 3, sl st in next sp on large motif, ch 3, dc in next 4 dc on Fill-in-motif, ch 3, tr in next 4 sps on large motif (2 preceding and 2 following joining), ch 3, dc in next 4 dc on Fill-in-motif, ch 3, sl st in next sp on large motif. Repeat from * around. Join. Fill in all sps between motifs in this manner.

The Petite Bedspread

The Petite Bedspread

Origianl Materials – Mercerized Crochet Cotton

Suggested Materials - Crochet Thread Size 10 or 12 – Optional - Use a Crochet Cotton if Preferred for a heavier bedspread

30 balls White and 10 balls color for Single Size;

37 balls White and 12 balls color for Double Size; or

48 balls White and 17 balls color for Single Size; 58 balls White and 21

balls color for Double Size; or

20 skeins White and 6 skeins color for Single Size; 24 skeins White and 8 skeins color for Double Size.

Single Size - 64 x 104 inches

Double Size - 90 x 104 inches

No. 10 Steel Crochet Hook.

GAUGE: Each Motif measures 214 inches across.

Work tightly for best results.

1st WHITE MOTIF: With White, (ch 9, sl st in one lp of 5th ch from hook for a p) 4 times to measure 1 3/4 inches.

Rnd 1: Remove hook from lp, insert it back in starting ch st, catch lp at other end-which was dropped and draw it thru ch st tightly to form a ring with the 4 ps on inside of chain-ring. Ch 1, hold starting thread end to left and working over it, (make sc at base of p, 7 sc in next sp between ps) 4 times, join with sl st in 1st 2 sc.

Rnd 2: Ch 5, sk 1 sc, dc in next sc, (ch 2, sk 1 sc, dc in next sc) 14 times, ch 2, join to 3d st of ch-5 (16 sps). This rnd will be slightly cupped.

Rnd 3: Ch 1, sc in same st, (ch 1, 3 dc in next sp, ch 1, sc in next dc) repeated around, join ch-1 to 1st sc.

Rnd 4: Sl st to center dc in next shell, ch 1, sc in same dc, * (ch 6, sc in center dc of next shell) twice, ch 4, (3 tr, ch 5, 3 tr) in back lp of center dc of next shell, ch 4, sc in both lps of center dc of next shell; repeat from * around, join to 1st sc.

Rnd 5: Ch 1, (2 sc, eh 4, 2 sc) across center of next 3 lps, * sc in 2d of next 3 tr, in corner lp make 2 sc, ch 4, 2 sc, *** ch 7, 2 sc, ch 4 and 2 sc; sc in 2d of next 3 tr, (2 sc, ch 4, 2 sc) across center of next 4 lps. Repeat from * around, join to 1st sc, cut with sewing end, thread to a needle and fasten off on back.

2d WHITE MOTIF: Repeat to *** in Rnd 5. Ch 3, sl st in one lp of center st of a corner p on 1st Motif, ch 3, 2 sc back in same lp of 2d Motif, ch 2, sl st in next p on 1st Motif, ch 2, 2 sc back in same lp of 2d Motif, sc in 2d of next 3 tr, (2 sc in center of next lp, ch 2, sl st in next p on 1st Motif, ch 2, 2 se back in same lp on 2d Motif) 4 times, sc in 2d of next 3 tr, 2 sc in corner lp, ch 2, sl st in next p on 1st Motif, ch 2, 2 sc back in same lp on 2d Motif, ch 3, sl st in one lp of center st of next (corner) p on 1st Motif, ch 3, (2 sc, ch 4, 2 sc) back in same lp on 2d Motif, sc in 2d of next 3 tr, (2 sc, ch 4, 2 sc) across center of next 4 sps. Complete Rnd beg. at * in Rnd 5.

COLORED MOTIF: Repeat Rnds 1, 2 and 3 with Sal. Rose marking final (16th) shell with a pin, cut with sewing end, thread to a needle and fasten off on back of one shell.

Rnd 4: Attach White to back lp of center dc of marked shell, ch 5 and working over starting thread end of White, make 2 tr, ch 5 and 3 tr in same st. * As for White Motif, ch 4, sc in next shell, (ch 6, sc in next shell) twice, ch 4, (3 tr, ch 5, 3 tr) in back lp of center dc of next shell (directly above a p in center ring). Repeat from * around, join final ch-4 to top of ch-5. Cut with 3" end.

Rnd 5: Attach Sal. Rose to center of one corner lp, ch 1 and working over starting Sal. Rose thread end, 1 sc in lp, ** (ch 7, 2 sc, ch 4, 2 sc) in bal. of lp, sc in 2d of next 3 tr, (2 sc, ch 4, 2 sc) across center of next 4 lps. Continue as for 1st White Motif beg. at * in Rnd 5, working over 3" White thread end. End Rnd with (2 sc, ch 4, 1 sc) in 1st corner lp and join to 1st sc. Fasten off.

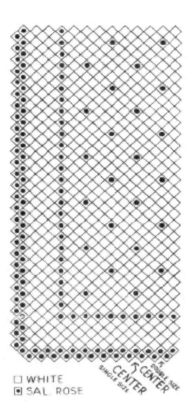

FOR SINGLE SIZE SPREAD, following Chart make 30 Colored Motifs to set into CENTER SECTION. Make a row of Colored Motifs for BORDER ROW outlining CENTER SECTION:- Make one Colored Motif. Make a 2d Motif as far as ** in Rnd 5. Ch 3, sl st in one lp of center st of a corner p on 1st Motif, ch 3, (2 sc, ch 4, 2 sc) back in bal. of corner lp on 2d Motif, sc in 2d of next 3 tr, (2 sc, ch 4, 2 sc) across center of next 4 lps. Complete Rnd as for 1st White Motif beg. at * in Rnd 5. Make 26 Colored Motifs, joining in same way by diagonally opposite corners into a straight row. Repeat for other side of BORDER. Then connect these 2 rows across bottom of CENTER SECTION with a row of 11 Colored Motifs. Now fill in CENTER SECTION with White Motifs and the 30 Colored Motifs always joining White Motifs to Colored Motifs, joining adjacent sides as 2d White Motif was joined to 1st Motif (where 4 corners meet, join 3d and 4th corners to joining of 1st 2 corners). Following Chart, make 2 rows of Colored Motifs for edge of 2 long sides and bottom end. Then connect these rows to BORDER ROW around CENTER SECTION with White Motifs.

FOR DOUBLE SIZE SPREAD, make and join 1039 White Motifs and 266 Colored Motifs as in Chart.

Stretch and pin spread right-side-down in true shape. Steam and press dry thru a doubled cloth.

TASSEL: Wind Sal. Rose 40 times around a 2 1/4 inch card. Cut at one edge, tie a 12 inch strand around center of strands, fold at tie, wrap a strand several times around tassel 3/8-inch from top and fasten. Trim Tassel to an even length. Fasten a tassel by the tie strings to each point around 3 sides of spread.

California Bedspread

California Bedspread

Original Materials Used – Mercerized Bedspread Cotton

Suggested Materials - Crochet Thread Size 10 or 12 – Optional - Use a Crochet Cotton if Preferred for a heavier bedspread. (Bedspread Cotton Yarn)

Single Size Spread-76 x 108 inches-70 balls of No. 1 White.

Double Size Spread-96 x 108 inches-80 balls of No. 1 White: or

Bedspread Cotton

Single Size Spread-76 x 108 inches-60 balls of No. 1 White.

Double Size Spread-96 x 108 inches-80 balls of No. 1 White.

Steel Crochet Hook No. 7.

GAUGE: Each motif measures 4 inches square.

FIRST MOTIF . . . Starting at center, ch 4.

1st rnd: 15 dc in 4th ch from hook. Join with sl st to top of starting chain.

2nd rnd: Ch 4, * dc in next dc, ch 1. Repeat from * around. Join to 3rd ch of ch-4.

3rd rnd: Sl st in next sp, ch 3, 4 dc in same sp, drop loop from hook, insert hook in top of ch-3 and draw dropped loop through (pc st made), * ch 3, 5 dc in next sp, drop loop from hook, insert hook in first dc of 5-dc group, draw dropped loop through (another pc st made). Repeat from * around, ending with ch 3. Join to tip of first pc st.

4th rnd: Sl st in next sp, sc in same sp. * (ch 5, sc in next sp) 3 times; ch 10, sc in next sp. Repeat from * around. Join.

5th rnd: Sl st in next loop, ch 3, pc st in same loop, * (ch 3, pc st in next loop) twice; ch 5, in next loop make 5 dc, ch 3 and 5 dc: ch 5, pc st in next loop. Repeat from * around. Join.

6th rnd: Sl st in next sp, ch 3, pc st in same sp, * ch 3, pc st in next sp, ch 5, 3 dc in next sp, dc in next 5 dc, in corner sp make 3 dc, ch 3 and 3 dc; dc in next 5 dc, 3 dc in next sp, ch 5, pc st in next sp. Repeat from * around. Join.

7th rnd: Sl st in next sp, ch 3, pc st in same sp, * ch 5, 3 dc in next sp, dc in next 6 dc, ch 7, in corner sp make sc, ch 11 and sc; ch 7, skip next 5 dc, dc in next 6 dc, 3 dc in next sp, ch 5. pc st in next sp. Repeat from * around. Join and break off.

SECOND MOTIF . . . Work as for First Motif until 6 rnds have been completed.

7th rnd: Sl st in next sp, ch 3, pc st in same sp, ch 5, 3 dc in next sp, dc in next 6 dc, ch 7, sc in corner sp, ch 5, sl st in corner loop on First Motif, ch 5, sc in same corner sp on Second Motif, ch 3, sl st in next loop on First Motif, ch 3, skip 5 dc on Second Motif, dc in next 6 dc, 3 dc in next sp, ch 2, sl st in next loop on First Motif, ch 2, pc st in next sp on Second Motif, ch 2, sl st in next loop on First Motif, ch 2, 3 dc in next sp on Second Motif, dc in next 6 dc, ch 3, sl st in next loop on First Motif, ch 3, sc in corner sp on Second Motif, ch 5, sl st in corner loop on First Motif, ch 5, sc in same corner sp on Second Motif. Complete rnd as for First Motif (no more joinings).

For Single Size Spread, make 18 rows of 27 motifs, joining adjacent sides as Second Motif was joined to First Motif (where 4 corners meet, join 3rd and 4th corners to joining of previous 2 corners).

For Double Size Spread, make 23 rows of 27 motifs.

BORDER ... 1st rnd: Attach thread to ch-11 loop on any corner motif, ch 3, in same loop make 4 dc, ch 5 and 5 dc; * 5 dc in next sp, ** dc in each dc across next group, dc in next 2 sps, dc in each dc across next group, 5 dc in each of next 4 sps. Repeat from ** across side to next ch-11 loop, in loop make 5 dc, ch 5 and 5 dc. Repeat from * around. Join.

2nd rnd: Ch 3, dc in each dc around, making 2 dc, ch 5 and 2 dc in each corner loop. Join.

3rd rnd: Sl st in next dc, ch 3, pc st in same dc, ch 2, skip 2 dc, pc st in next dc, ch 2, in next corner sp make pc st, ch 5 and pc st; * ch 2, skip 2 dc, pc st in next dc. Repeat from * around, working other corners as before. Join.

4th rnd: Sl st in next sp, ch 3, 2 dc in same sp, 3 dc in each sp around, making 3 dc, ch 5 and 3 dc in each corner sp. Join and break off.

FRINGE . . . Cut 10 strands of thread, each 45 inches long, twist these strands tightly, then double and give them a twist in the opposite direction, make a knot 1 inch from one end. Fold cord in half and draw looped end through sp between first and 2nd dc on long side of spread, draw loose ends through loop and pull up tightly. Tie a knot 1 inch from other end. Cut cord at ends and unravel loose ends to form fringe. Make necessary number of fringe the same way, spacing them evenly apart. Block to measurements.

Filet Block Bedspread

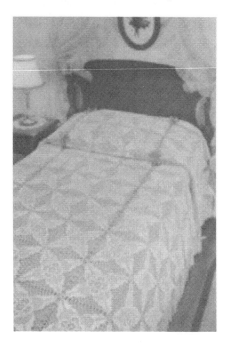

Filet Block Bedspread

Original Materials Used - Bedspread Cotton - A soft, strong, long-lasting bedspread cotton for crocheted and knitted spreads. Ecru, White, and Cream balls.

Suggested Materials - Crochet Thread Size 10 or 12 – Optional - Use a Crochet Cotton if Preferred for a heavier bedspread

NO. 11 FILET BLOCK

BEDSPREAD

MATERIALS - Bedspread Cotton Art.155 in White, Cream or Ecru (300 and 250 yard balls):

Single size-36 balls

Double size - 38 balls

GAUGE - Each Block measures about 8" square.

For single size spread about 72"x l04" without fringe, make 9 x 13 Blocks;

For double size spread about 80"x l04", make 10 x 13 Blocks.

Crochet hook size 10.

15-yds. ribbon 5/8" wide.

This Pattern is worked from the center out

BLOCK-Ch 6, sl st in 1st st. Ch 11, tr in ring, (ch 5, tr in ring) 6 times, ch 2, dc in 6th st of 1st 11-ch.

ROW 2-Ch 3, turn, 2 dc in 2-ch sp, * dc in tr, 5 dc in 5-ch, dc in tr, (3 dc, ch 5, 3 dc) in corner 5-ch. Repeat from * around. End with 3 dc in end sp, ch 2, dc in top of 1st 3-ch.

ROW 3-Ch 3, turn, 2 dc in 2-ch sp, * dc in next dc, ch 6, sc in next 6th dc, ch 6, dc in next 6th dc, (3 dc, ch 5, 3 dc) in corner 5-ch. Repeat from * around. End as in last row.

ROW 4-Ch 5, turn, * dc in next 4 dc, ch 7, sc in next sc, ch 7, flc in next 4 dc, ch 2, (dc, ch 5, dc) in 3d st of corner 5-ch, ch 2 and repeat from * around. End with ch 2, dc in 3d st of 1st 5-ch.

ROW 5-Ch 5, turn, * dc in next dc, ch 2, dc in next 4 dc, 3 dc in next lp, ch 2, tr down in sc, ch 2, 3 dc in next lp, dc in 4 dc, ch 2, dc in next dc, ch 2, (dc, ch 5, dc) in 3d st of corner 5-ch lp, ch 2 and repeat from * around. End as in last row.

ROW 6-Ch 5, turn, dc in next dc and following Chart, make 3 sps, (4 bls, 4 sps, a 5-ch corner sp, 4 sps) repeated around. End as in Row 4.

ROW 7-Ch 5, turn, dc in next dc and follow Chart around. End as in Row 4.

ROW 8-Ch 3, turn, 2 bls, * 4 sps, 1 bl, ch 5, dc in next 6th dc, 1 bl, 4 sps, 1 bl, (3 dc, ch 5, 3 dc) in corner sp, dc in dc, 1 bl. Repeat from * around. End as in Row 2.

ROW 9-Ch 3, turn, 7 bls, * ch 5, dc in next 5-ch sp, ch 5, dc in next 4th dc, 6 bls, (3 dc, ch 5, 3 dc) in corner sp, dc in dc, 6 bis. Repeat from * around. End as in Row 2.

ROW 10-Ch 3, turn and continue as in Chart. Repeat for Row 11.

ROW 12-Ch 3, turn, 2 dc in 2-ch, * dc in 4 dc, ch 6, sl st in side-top of last dc for a p, dc in next 3 dc, ch 8, sc thru 2 lps of 7th ch st from hook for a p, ch 2 (a p-lp made), dc in next 6th dc, (a p-lp, dc in next 5-ch sp) 6 times, a p-lp, dc in next 4th dc, a p-lp, sk 5 dc, dc in next 4 dc, ch 6, sl st in last dc for a p, dc in next 3 dc, 3 dc in corner sp, a 6-ch p, ch 9, sc thru 2 lps of 8th ch st from hook for a p, ch 2, ** (1 dc, a 6-ch p and 2 dc) in same corner sp. Repeat from * around, ending at **. Sl st in top of 1st 3-ch, ch 6, sl st in same st. Cut 6" long, thread to a needle and fasten off on back.

2nd BLOCK-Join to 1st Block while making Row 12:-At corners, in place of 9-ch, make 5-ch, sl st in one lp of st at end of a corner p on 1st Block, ch 3, sk last 3 sts of 5-ch, sc back thru 2 lps of next ch st to complete joining p, ch 2, dc in corner sp, ch 3, sl st in next p on 1st Block, ch 3, sl st back in last dc, 2 dc in same corner sp, dc in next 4 dc, ch 3, sl st in next p on 1st Block, ch 3, sl st back in last dc, dc in next 3 dc, ch 5, sl st in next p on 1st Block, ch 3, sk last 3 sts of 5-ch, sc back thru 2 lps of next ch st, ch 2, dc in next 6th dc. Continue to join the next 10 ps to corresponding ps on 1st Block in same way, then join the corners as given above.

Continue to make and join Blocks for desired size. Block to measurements given.

FRINGE-Wind 2 strands 5 times around a card 8" wide. Cut at one edge. Fold strands in center, insert a large crochet hook up from underneath thru a p on edge of spread, catch lp of strands and pull thru, pass ends of strands thru lp and pull tight. Repeat in each p around both sides and bottom of spread.

Lace ribbon thru beading rows between Blocks and trim with rosettes as illustrated.

Italian Rose Bedspread

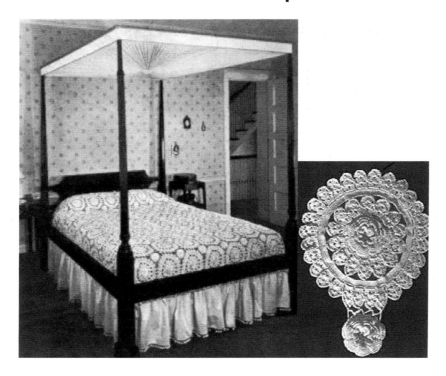

Italian Rose Bedspread

Size - 92" x 108"

Crochet Cotton, 22 cones (800 yds) Ecru or White

Suggested Materials - Crochet Thread Size 10 or 12 – Optional - Use a Crochet Cotton if Preferred for a heavier bedspread

Crochet Hook Size 7

Round 1: Ch 9, join to form ring.

Round 2: * Ch 5, sl st in next ch, and repeat from * around (7 loops).

Round 3: * 7 dc over ch 5, sl st in sl st, and repeat from * (7 petals).

Round 4: * Ch 6, sl st in sl st and repeat from *.

Round 5: * 8 dc over ch 6, sl st between petals, and repeat from *.

Round 6: * Ch 6, sl st in sl st and repeat from *.

Round 7: Repeat Round 5.

Round 8: * Ch 7, sl st in sl st, and repeat from *.

Round 9: * 9 dc over ch 7, sl st between petals, and repeat from *.

Round 10: * Ch 8, sl st in sl st and repeat from *.

Round 11: * 10 dc over ch 8, sl st between petals, and repeat from *.

Round 12: * Ch 6, sl st in 5th dc, ch 6, sl st between petals, and repeat from *.

Round 13: * Ch 3, 3 dc over ch 6, ch 3, 3 dc same ch, and repeat from * ending round with ch 3; Join.

Round 14: Ch 3, * 3 dc over ch 3, ch 3; 3 dc over same ch, ch 5, and repeat from * ending with ch 3, join.

Round 15: * Ch 3, 3 dc over ch 3, ch 3, 3 dc over same ch, ch 3, sl st over first and second ch, and repeat from *.

Round 16: Sl st in each ch to center of ch 3 of shell * ch 12, sl st over cent of ch 3, and repeat from *.

Rounds 17 to 21 incl.: Single crochet in each stitch.

Round 22: * Ch 6, sl st into center of band between shells (about 7th or 8th sc), ch 6, sl st opposite where shell joins band, and repeat from *. Round 23: Repeat Round 13.

Round 24: Repeat Round 14.

Round 25: Repeat Round 15.

CONNECTING SMALL ROSE MEDALLION:

Rounds 1 to 11 incl.: (7 petals to round),

TO JOIN:

Work 4 large medallions. Join with sl st connecting 4 shells of large medallion with 4 shells of another large medallion, skip 4 shells and join another large medallion, and repeat having 4 large medallions joined at start. Join Small Medallion as follows: * Ch 5, sl st into center of first shell on large medallion, ch 5, sl st into center of rose petal of small medallion, ch 5, sl st into next shell on large medallion, ch 5, sl st between petals of small medallion and repeat from *.

NOTE- An edging is not required as medallions form edge.

Grandma's Garden Bedspread

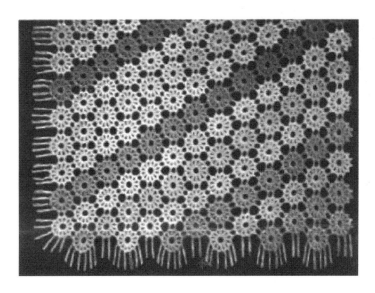

Grandma's Garden Bedspread

For a spread 84x108 inches it takes 972 flowerets, having 26 Flowerets on 1st row, 28 on second row and requires 36 balls of Knitting & Crochet Cotton.

Suggested Materials - Crochet Cotton

DIRECTIONS

Knitting & Crochet Cotton, and #3 Crochet Hook.

Flowerets: Wind thread around 2 fingers 6 times (this makes a ring about 7/8"}.

1st rnd: 36 sc in ring, join with sl st.

2nd row: Ch 5, 1 d tr c (thread over hook 3 times, taking off 2 loops at a time) next 2 sts, * ch 3, 1 d tr c next 3 sts, repeat from * around ring having 12 petals, join with sl st.

3rd rnd: * 1 sc in middle d tr c, 3 dc next ch loop, 1 p (use 4 ch) 3 dc in same ch loop, repeat from * around ring, fasten off.

To join Flowerets: For 1st row, on 3rd rnd of 2nd floweret, complete 10 p, * 1 sc in middle of d tr c, 3 dc next ch loop, ch 2, insert hook thru p of 1st floweret, ch 2, sl st in last dc, 3 dc in same ch loop, repeat from * once more, fasten off. On the 3rd floweret join 2 p at opposite side of 2nd floweret, leaving 4 p between. Continue same from other flowerets across top of article.

2nd row: Start from right to left; after 8 p are made on last rnd of floweret, leave 8 p of floweret on 1st row, join next 2 p with 9th and 10th p, and last 2 p of same floweret with 2 p of 2nd floweret of 1st row, * after 6 p are made on next floweret, leave 6 p of 1st floweret, join next 2 p to 2 p of 1st floweret, join next 2 p with 2 p of 2nd floweret of 1st row, join last 2 p to 2 p of 3rd floweret of 1st row, repeat from * to end of row.

3rd row: Start from right to left, after 10 p are made, leave 2 p of 1st floweret on 2nd row, join next 2 p, * after 6 p are made on next floweret, leave 8 p of 1st floweret, join next 2 p, join next 2 p with last 2 p of 1st floweret of 2nd row, join last 2 p with next 2 p of 2nd floweret. Repeat from * across.

Repeat 2nd and 3rd rows alternately for as many rows as desired.

Add fringe if desired.

Pineapple Pinwheel Bedspread

Pineapple Pinwheel Bedspread

Mercerized Cotton Size 30 or

Suggested Materials - Crochet Thread Size 10 or 12 or size of your choice – Optional - Use a Crochet Cotton if Preferred for a heavier bedspread

For Single Size - 71 1/2 x 104 inches (excluding fringe)

A. 104 - 86 balls (White, Ecru or Cream)

B. 34 - 62 balls (White, Ecru or Cream)

B. 345 - 36 balls (White or Ecru only)

For Double Size - 91 x 104 inches (excluding fringe)

A. 104 - 107 balls (White, Ecru or Cream)

B. 34 - 77 balls (White, Ecru or Cream)

B. 345 - 45 balls (White or Ecru only)

Steel Crochet Hook No. 10.

Motif measures 6 1/2 inches square.

MOTIF . . . Starting at center, ch 5.

1st rnd: 15 tr in 5th ch from hook. Join with sl st to top of ch-5 (16 tr, counting starting chain as 1 tr).

2nd rnd: Ch 3, in same place as sl st was made, make dc, ch 3 and 2 dc; (ch 1, skip next tr, in next tr make 2 dc, ch 3 and 2 dc) 7 times; ch 1. Join to top of ch-3.

3rd rnd: Sl st in next 6 sts and in next ch-1 sp, ch 3, in same sp make dc, ch 1 and 2 dc (starting shell made); * ch 2, dc in next loop, ch 2, in next sp make 2 dc, ch 1 and 2 dc (shell made). Repeat from * around, ending with ch 2. Join to top of ch-3.

4th and 5th rnds: Sl st in next dc and in following sp, ch 3 and complete a starting shell in same sp (starting shell over shell made), * ch 3, dc in next dc, ch 3, shell in next shell sp (shell over shell made). Repeat from * around, ending with ch 3. Join as before.

6th rnd: * Shell over shell, ch 2, in next dc make tr, 6 dc and tr (start of pineapple), ch 2. Repeat from * around. Join.

7th rnd: * Shell over shell, ch 1, dc in next tr, (ch 1, dc in next st) 7 times; ch 1. Repeat from * around. Join.

8th rnd: * Shell over shell, skip next sp, (ch 1, 4 dc in next sp, drop loop from hook, insert hook in first dc of 4-dc group and draw dropped loop through - pc st made) 7 times; ch 1. Repeat from * around. Join.

9th rnd: * Shell over shell, skip next sp, (ch 3, sc in next sp between pc sts) 6 times; ch 3. Repeat from * around. Join.

10th rnd: * Shell over shell, ch 1, 2 dc in same shell sp (double shell made), ch 4, skip next sp, (pc st in next loop, ch 1) 4 times, pc st in next loop; ch 4. Repeat from * around. Join.

11th rnd: * Shell in first sp of double shell, ch 3, shell in second sp of same double shell, ch 5, (sc in next ch-1 sp, ch 3) 3 times; sc in next sp, ch 5. Repeat from * around. Join.

12th rnd: * Shell over shell, ch 3, in next sp make dc, ch 3 and dc (V st made); ch 3, shell over shell, ch 5, (pc st in next ch-3 loop, ch 1) twice, pc st in next loop; ch 5. Repeat from * around. Join.

13th rnd: * Shell over shell, ch 4, V st in next V-st sp (V st over V st made); ch 4, shell over shell, ch 4, sc in next ch-1 sp, ch 3, se in next sp, ch 4. Repeat from * around. Join.

14th rnd: * Shell over shell, ch 5, V st over V st, ch 5, shell over shell, ch 3, pc st in next ch-3 loop, ch 3. Repeat from * around. Join.

15th rnd: * Shell over shell, ch 5, sc in next dc, ch 3, sc in next dc (ch 5, shell over shell) twice; ch 5, in next dc make 2 tr, ch 1 and 2 tr (tr shell made); ch 3, in next V-st sp make tr, ch 3 and tr (tr-V st made), ch 3, tr shell in next dc, ch 5, dc shell over shell, ch 5. Repeat from * around. Join.

16th rnd: * Dc shell over shell, ch 7, sc in next sc, ch 5, sc in next sc, ch 7, dc shell over shell, ch 3, shell over shell, ch 5, tr shell over tr shell, ch 3, tr in next sp, ch 3, tr-V st over tr-V st, ch 3, tr in next ch-3 sp, ch 3, tr shell over tr shell, ch 5, dc shell over shell, ch 3. Repeat from * around. Join.

17th rnd: * Shell over shell, ch 9, sc in next sc, ch 6, sc in next sc, ch 9, (shell over shell) twice; ch 5, tr shell over tr shell, (ch 3, tr in next sp) twice; ch 3, tr-V st over tr-V st, (ch 3, tr in next sp) twice; ch 3, tr shell over tr shell; ch 5, shell over shell. Repeat from * around. Join.

18th rnd: Sl st to center of shell, ch 4, tr in same place, * ch 13, sc in next sc, ch 7, sc in next sc, ch 13, holding back on hook the last loop of each tr, (2 tr in next shell sp) twice, thread over and draw through all loops on hook (cluster made); ch 5, tr shell over tr shell, (ch 3, tr in next sp) 3 times; ch 3, tr-V st over tr-V st, (ch 3, tr in next sp) 3 times; ch 3, tr shell over tr shell, ch 5, cluster over next 2 shells. Repeat from * around, ending with a 2-tr cluster in last shell. Join to first tr. Break off.

Make 11 rows of 16 motifs for Single Size Spread, or 14 rows of 16 motifs for Double size.

With wrong side facing, sew or sc motifs neatly together.

FRINGE . . . Cut 20 strands 8 inches long for each fringe. Working along first long side, make a fringe in corner V-st sp; * (make 1 fringe in next sp, skip next sp) twice; make 1 fringe in next shell sp, and in following loop, (make 2 fringes in next loop, make 1 fringe in next loop) twice; make 1 fringe in next shell sp, skip 1 sp, (make 1 fringe in next sp, skip next sp) 3 times. Repeat from * around 3 sides of spread.

Popcorn Star Bedspread

Popcorn Star Bedspread

Original Materials Bedspread Cotton, 43 balls of White, or 32 balls of Ecru for double size spread; 34 balls of White, or 25 balls of Ecru for single size spread.

Suggested Materials - Crochet Thread Size 10 or 12 or size of your choice – Optional - Use a Crochet Cotton if Preferred for a heavier bedspread

Steel crochet hook No. 8 or 9.

GAUGE: Each motif measures about 6 1/2 inches across, from side to side.

For a double size spread, 91 x 116 inches, make 256 motifs.

For a single size spread, 72 x 116 inches, make 199 motifs.

MOTIF...Starting ar center, ch 8, join with sl st to form ring.

1st rnd: Ch 5 (always to count as dc), 17 dc in ring. Join with sl st to 3rd st of ch-3 first made.

2nd rnd: Ch 4 (to count as dc and ch-1), dc in same place as sl st, * ch 3, skip 2 dc; in next dc make dc, ch 1, dc. Repeat from * around, ending with ch-3, sl st in 3rd St of ch-4 first made.

3rd rnd: Sl st in 1st ch-1 sp, ch 3, 4 dc in same sp, * ch 3, 5 dc in next ch-1 sp. Repeat from * around, ending with ch 3, sl st in 3rd st of ch-3 first made.

4th rnd: Ch 3, dc in same place as sl st, * dc in each of next 3 dc; in next dc make a pc st (to make a pc st ch 1, 5 dc in next st, drop st from hook, insert hook back in ch-1 and draw loop through the one on hook); ch 1, dc in same st where pc st was made, ch 3, 2 dc in 1st dc of next dc-group. Repeat from * around, ending with ch 3, sl st in 3rd st of ch-3 first made.

5th rnd: Ch 3, dc in same place as sl st, * dc in each of next 3 dc; pc st in next dc, ch 2, pc st in next ch-1 sp, ch 1, dc in same sp, ch 3, 2 dc in 1st dc of next dc-group. Repeat from * around, ending with ch 3, sl st in 3rd st of ch-3 first made.

6th rnd: Ch 3, dc in same place as sl st, * dc in each of next 3 dc, pc st in next dc, ch 2, pc st in next sp between pc sts; ch 2, pc st in next ch-1 sp ch 1, dc in same sp as last pc st, ch 3, 2 dc in 1st dc of next dc-group. Repeat from * around, ending with ch 3, sl st in 3rd st of ch-3 first made.

7th rnd: Ch 3, dc in same place as sl st, * dc in each of next 3 dc, pc st in next dc, ch 2, pc st in next ch-2 sp between pc sts; ch 2, pc st in next ch-2 sp between pc sts, ch 2, pc st in ch-1 sp, ch 1, dc in same sp as last pc st, ch 3, 2 dc in 1st dc of next dc-group. Repeat from * around, ending with ch 3, sl st in 3rd st of ch-3 first made.

8th rnd: Ch 3, dc in same place as sl st, * dc in each of next 3 dc, pc st in next dc, ch 2, pc st in next ch-2 sp between pc sts, ch 2, pc st in next ch-2 sp, ch 2, pc st in next ch-2 sp, ch 2, pc st in ch-1 sp, ch 1, dc in same sp, ch 3, 2 dc in 1st dc of next dc-group. Repeat from * around, ending with ch-3, sl st in 3rd st of ch-3 first made.

9th rnd: Sl st in next dc, ch 3, dc in each of next 3 dc, * dc in next pc st, pc st in next ch-2 sp between pc sts, ch 2, pc st in next ch-2 sp, ch 2, pc sr in next ch-2 sp, ch 2, pc st in next ch-2 sp, ch 1, dc in same sp, ch 5, sc in next ch-3 sp, ch 5, skip 1 dc, dc in each of next 4 dc. Repeat from * around, ending with ch 5, sc in last ch-3 sp, ch 5, sl st in 3rd st of ch-3 first made.

10th rnd: Sl st in next dc, ch 3, dc in each of next 3 dc, * dc in next pc st, pc st in next ch-2 sp between pc sts, ch 2, pc st in next ch-2 sp, ch 2, pc st in next ch-2 sp, ch 1, dc in same sp as last pc st, ch 5, sc in next ch-5 loop, ch 5, sc in next loop, ch 5, skip 1 dc, dc in each of next 4 dc. Repeat from * around, ending with ch 5, sc in next loop, ch 5, sc in next loop, ch 5, sl st in 3rd st of ch-3 first made.

11th rnd: Sl st in next dc, ch 3, dc in each of next 3 dc, * dc in next pc st, pc st in next ch-2 sp between pc sts, ch 2, pc st in next ch-2 sp, ch 1, dc in same place as last pc st, ch 5, sc in next loop; in next loop make 3 dc, ch 3, 3 dc; sc in next loop, ch 5, skip 1 dc, dc in each of next 4 dc. Repeat from * around, ending with ch 5, sl st in 3rd st of ch-3 first made.

12th rnd: Sl st in next dc, ch 3, dc in each of next 3 dc, * dc in next pc st, pc st in next ch-2 sp between pc sts, ch 1, dc in same sp as last pc st, ch 5, sc in next loop, dc in next sc, dc in each of next 3 dc; in next ch-3 sp make 2 dc, ch 3, 2 dc; dc in each of next 3 dc, dc in next sc, sc in next loop, ch 5, skip 1 dc, dc in each of next 4 dc. Repeat from * around, ending with ch 5, sl st in 3rd st of ch-3 first made.

13th rnd: Sl st in next dc, ch 3, dc in each of next 3 dc, holding back the last loop of each dc on hook, dc in ch-1 sp, holding back last loop of dc as before; thread over and draw through all loops on hook, ch 1 to fasten (1 cluster made), * ch 6, sc in next loop, dc in next sc, dc in each of next 6 dc; in ch-3 sp make 2 dc, ch 3, 2 dc; dc in each of next 6 dc, dc in next sc, sc in next loop, ch 6, skip 1 dc, dc in each of next 4 dc, holding back the last loop of each dc on hook; dc in ch-1 sp, holding back last loop as before. Thread over and draw through all loops on hook, ch 1 to fasten (another cluster made). Repeat from * around, ending with ch 6, sl st in tip of 1st cluster made.

14th rnd: * Sl st in each of next 3 ch, sc in same loop, dc in next sc, dc in each dc across to within next ch-3 sp; in ch-3 sp make 2 dc, ch 3, 2 dc; dc in each dc across to within next sc, dc in sc, sc in next loop, sl st in each of last 3 ch of next ch-6, sl st at tip of cluster. Repeat from * around. Fasten and break off.

Make necessary number of blocks, and sew together on wrong side with neat over-and-over stitches, as in diagram (for single size spread, disregard motifs to left of heavy line).

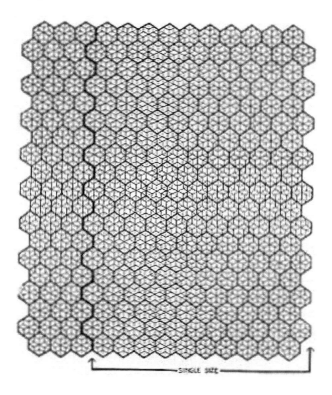

Star Popcorn Bedspread

Star Popcorn Bedspread

Make separate sections at your leisure and join them into a bedspread of any desired size.

Approximate Size 85 inches by 103 inches. (For a Full Double Bed Size)

To make a full-size double bedspread use:

36 skeins of Ivory or White Crochet and Knitting Cotton, Article 50, or 54 skeins of any desired color.

Suggested Materials - Crochet Thread Size 10 or 12 or heavier - or Optional Crochet Cotton if Preferred for a heavier bedspread.

1 Steel Crochet Hook, Standard Size 5.

Gauge: 8 stitches - 1 inch. 4 rows - 1 inch.

This bedspread is made up of squares, sewn together. Each square should measure about 14 1/2 inches.

Squares-Ch 8, join with a slip st into a ring.

1st round: ch 6, 3 dc in ring, ch 3, 3 dc in ring, ch 3, 3 dc in ring, ch 3, 2 dc in ring, join with a slip st in 3rd st of chain at beginning of round,

1 sc in space made by same chain.

2nd round: ch 6, 2 dc in same space as the sc, 1 dc in each of the next 3 dc, * 2 dc in next space, ch 3, 2 dc in same space, 1 dc in each of the next 3 dc; repeat from * twice, then 1 dc in same space as the sc at beginning of round, 1 slip st in 3rd st of ch 6, and 1 sc in space made by same chain.

3rd round: ch 6, 2 dc in same space as the sc, 1 dc in each of the next 3 dc, then make a "popcorn" st, as follows: 5 dc in next dc, drop loop from hook, insert this in top of first dc and draw the dropped loop through, tighten loop; * 1 dc in each of the next 3 dc, 2 dc in next space, ch 3, 2 dc in same space, 1 dc in each of the next 3 dc, 1 popcorn in next dc; repeat from * twice; 1 dc in each of the next 2 dc, 1 dc in the joining slip st, 1 dc in same space as the sc at beginning of round, 1 slip st in 3rd st of ch 6, and 1 sc in space made by same chain; end each round in the same way.

4th round: ch 6, 2 dc in same space as the sc, 1 dc in each of the next 3 dc, 1 popcorn, 1 dc in each of the next 3 sts (the center of these dc is made in top of the popcorn), 1 popcorn, 1 dc in each of the next 3 dc, 2 dc in next space, ch 3, 2 dc in same space; continue in same way on the next 3 sides of square and end as in 3rd round.

5th round: ch 6, 2 dc in same space as the sc, 1 dc in each of the next 3 dc, 1 popcorn, 3 dc, 1 popcorn, 3 dc, 1 popcorn, 3 dc, 2 dc in next space, ch 3, 2 dc in same space; continue in same way on the next 3 sides of square, and end as in 3rd round.

6th round: ch 6, 2 dc in same space as the sc, 1 dc in each of the next 3 dc, 1 popcorn, 3 dc, 1 popcorn, 3 dc, 1 popcorn, 3 dc, 1 popcorn, 3 dc, 2 dc in next space, ch 3, 2 dc in same space; continue in this way on the remaining 3 sides and end as in 3rd round.

7th round: ch 6, 2 dc in space below, 3 dc on the next 3 dc, 1 popcorn, 3 dc, 1 popcorn, 3 dc, 1 popcorn, 3 dc, 1 popcorn, 3 dc, 1 popcorn, 3 dc, 2 dc in next space, ch 3, 2 dc in same space; continue on remaining 3 sides and end as in 3rd round.

8th round: ch 6, 2 dc in space, 3 dc, 1 popcorn, 3 dc, 1 popcorn, 3 dc, 1 popcorn, 3 dc, 1 popcorn, 3 dc, 1 popcorn, 3 dc, 1 popcorn, 3 dc, 2 dc in next space, ch 2, 2 dc in same space; continue on remaining 3 sides, and end as in 3rd round.

9th round: ch 6, 2 dc in space, 1 dc in each of the next 7 sts, 1 popcorn, 3 dc, 1 popcorn, 3 dc, 1 popcorn, 3 dc, 1 popcorn, 3 dc, 1 popcorn, 7 dc, 2 dc in next space, ch 3, 2 dc in same space; continue on remaining 3 sides, and end as in 3rd round.

10th round: ch 6, 2 dc in space, 1 dc in each of the next 11 sts, 1 popcorn, 3 dc, 1 popcorn, 3 dc, 1 popcorn, 3 dc, 1 popcorn, 11 dc, 2 dc in next space, ch 3, 2 dc in same space, continue in same way on remaining 3 sides, and end as in 3rd round.

11th round: ch 6, 2 dc in space, 1 dc in each of the next 15 sts, 1 popcorn, 3 dc, 1 popcorn, 3 dc, 1 popcorn, 15 dc, 2 dc in next space, ch 3, 2 dc in same space; end as in 3rd round.

12th round: ch 6, 2 dc in space, 1 dc in each of the next 19 sts, 1 popcorn, 3 dc, 1 popcorn, 19 dc, 2 dc in next space, ch 3, 2 dc in same space; end as in 3rd round.

13th round: ch 6, 2 dc in space, 1 dc in each of the next 23 sts, 1 popcorn, 23 dc, 2 dc in next space, ch 3, 2 dc in same space; end as in 3rd round.

14th round: ch 6, 2 dc in space, 1 dc in each st (51 dc) to next space, 2 dc in space, ch 3, 2 dc in same space, end as in 3rd round.

15th round: ch 6, 1 dc in same space, ch 1, 1 dc in same space, * ch 1, skip first dc below, 1 dc in next dc; repeat from * to next corner space, ch 1, 1 dc in space, ch 1, 1 more dc in same space, ch 3, 1 dc in same space, ch 1, 1 more dc in same space; continue in same way on remaining 3 sides, working all corners alike; end with 1 dc in last corner space, ch 1, 1 slip st in 3rd st of ch 6, 1 sc in next space.

16th round: ch 6, 2 dc in space, * 1 dc in next dc, 1 dc under next ch 1; repeat from * to next corner space, 2 dc in this space, ch 3, 2 dc in same space; continue in same way on remaining 3 sides, and end as in 3rd round.

17th round: ch 6, 2 dc in space, 1 dc in each of the next 2 dc, 1 popcorn and 3 dc, alternately, to within 2 dc of next corner space (16 popcorns in row), 1 dc in each of the last 2 dc, 2 dc in corner space, ch 3, 2 dc in same space; continue in same way on remaining 3 sides; end as in 3rd round.

18th round: same as 17th round, having 17 popcorns on each side of square.

19th round: ch 6, 2 dc in space, 1 dc in each st to next corner space, 2 dc in corner space, ch 3, 2 more dc in same space; continue in this way on remaining 3 sides, end as in 3rd round.

20th round: same as 15th round.

21st round: same as 16th round.

22nd round: ch 6, 2 dc in space, 1 dc in each of the next 2 dc, 1 popcorn and 3 dc, alternately, until there are 6 popcorns, 41 dc on the next 41 dc, 1 popcorn and 3 dc, alternately, until there are 6 popcorns, 1 dc in each of the remaining 2 dc to corner space, 2 dc in space, ch 3, 2 more dc in same space; continue in same way on remaining 3 sides and end as in 3rd round.

23rd round: follow directions for 22nd round until there are 6 popcorns from first corner, 1 dc in each of the next 45 dc, 6 popcorns with 3 dc between each, 2 dc to next corner space, 2 dc in space, ch 3, 2 more dc in same space; continue in same way to end of round and join as before.

24th round: same as 23rd round, but with 49 dc between the popcorn motifs.

25th round: same as 23rd round, but with 53 dc between the popcorn motifs.

26th round: same as 23rd round, but with 57 dc between popcorn motifs.

27th round: same as 23rd round, but with 61 dc between popcorn motifs.

28th round: same as 19th round.

29th round: same as 15th round. This completes the square.

Make 35 squares and sew them together, 7 in length and 5 in width, working from wrong side and taking up top threads only of edge sts; becareful to have corners meet exactly; use the same thread as for crocheting.

Work 2 rows of meshes around the entire spread, as follows: 1 sc in space just before a corner, ch 5, 1 sc in corner space, ch 5, 1 sc in next space, * ch 5, skip 1 space, 1 sc in next space; repeat from * to next corner; continue in this way on remaining 3 sides, working all corners the same as first.

2nd row: 1 sc in first space, * ch 5, 1 sc in next space, repeat from * around.

Fringe-Wind thread around an 8-inch cardboard; cut at one end. Tie 2 fringes of 5 strands each, in each space; tie 2 and 2 fringes together about 1/2 inch below first knots; knot a 3rd time 3/4 of an inch below last knot, tying half the number of strands of one knot with half the strands of next knot. (See picture).

Beauty Rose Bedspread

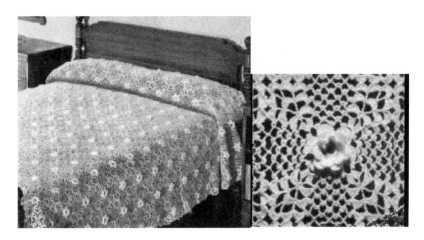

Beauty Rose Bedspread

Original Materials - Lustersheen, 55 skeins of White or Ecru, or 74 skeins of any color for double size spread; 46 skeins of White or Ecru, or 62 skeins of any color for single size spread.

Suggested Materials - Crochet Thread Size 10 or 12 or preferred size – Optional - Use a Crochet Cotton if Preferred for a heavier bedspread

Steel crochet hook No. 7.

GAUGE: Each block measures about 5 inches square.

For a double size spread, 90 x 110 inches, make 18 x 22 blocks. For a single size spread, 75 x 110 inches, make 15 x 22 blocks.

FIRST BLOCK...Starring at center, ch 12 and join with sl st to form ring.

1st rnd: Ch 1, 24 sc in ring. Join with sl st in 1st sc made.

2nd rnd: * Ch 5, skip 3 sc, sc in next sc. Repeat from * around, ending with sc at base of ch-5 first made (6 loops).

3rd rnd: In each ch-5 loop make: 1 sc, 1 half dc, 5 dc, 1 half dc, 1 sc (6 petals).

4th rnd: Sl st in each st to center sc under 1st loop, * ch 5, sc in center sc under next loop. Repeat from * around, ending with sl st at base of ch-5 first made.

5th rnd: In each ch-5 loop make: 1 sc, 1 half dc, 1 dc, 5 tr, 1 dc, 1 half dc, 1 sc.

6th rnd: * Ch 7, skip 1 petal, sc in back of next sc of previous loop row. Repeat from * around.

7th rnd: In each ch-7 loop make: 1 sc, 1 half dc, 1 dc, 7 tr, 1 dc, 1 half dc, 1 sc.

8th rnd: Sl st to 1st tr of next petal, * ch 5, skip 5 tr, sc in next tr, ch 3, sc in same tr, ch 5, sc in 1st tr of next petal, ch 3, sc in same tr. Repeat from * around.

9th rnd: Sl st in 1st loop, ch 4 (to count as tr), 2 tr in same loop, ** ch 3, 3 tr in same loop, * ch 5; in next loop make: sc, ch 3, sc. Repeat from * once more, ch 5, 3 tr in next ch-5 loop. Repeat from ** around, ending with ch 2, dc in 4th st of ch-4 first made.

10th rnd: * Ch 5; sc, ch 3, sc in next loop. Repeat from * around,

11th rnd: ** In next loop make: 1 sc, 1 half dc, 5 dc, 1 half dc, 1 sc (a shell made); sc in next ch-3 loop, in next ch-5 loop make another shell as before; * ch 5; sc, ch 3. sc in next loop. Repeat from * once more, ch 5. Then repeat from ** around.

12th rnd: Sl st in each st to center dc of next shell, ** ch 5; in the sc between shells make: tr, ch 5, tr; ch 5, sc in center dc of next shell, * ch 5, sc, ch 3, sc in next loop. Repeat from * 2 more times, ch 5, sc in center dc of next shell. Repeat from ** around.

13th rnd: ** In each of next 3 loops make a shell as before; sc in next loop, ch 3, sc in same loop, * ch 5, sc, ch 3, sc in next loop. Repeat from * 2 more times. Then repeat from ** around.

14th rnd: Sl st to center dc of next shell, ** ch 5, dc between this and next shell, ch 5; in 3rd dc of center shell make: tr, ch 5, tr; ch 5, dc between this and next shell, ch 5, sc in center dc of 3rd shell, * ch 5, sc, ch 3, sc in next loop. Repeat from * 2 more times, ch 5, sc in center dc of next shell. Repeat from ** around.

15th rnd: ** Make a shell in each of next 5 loops; sc, ch 3, sc in next loop; * ch 5, sc, ch 3, sc in next loop. Repeat from * 2 more times. Then repeat from ** around. Fasten and break off.

SECOND BLOCK...Work exactly as for first block to l4th rnd incl.

15th rnd: Make a shell in each of next 2 loops; in corner loop make: 1 sc, 1 half dc, 4 dc, sc in corresponding dc of corner shell of first block (always keeping right side of work on top), and complete shell on second block as before. * In next loop make: 1 sc, 1 half dc, 2 dc, sc in 3rd dc of corresponding shell on first block, and complete shell as before. Repeat from * once more. In next loop make sc, ch 3, sc; ** ch 2, sc in corresponding loop of first block, ch 2, sc in next loop back on second block, ch 3, sc in same loop. Repeat from ** 2 more times. *** In next ch-5 loop on second block make: 1 sc, 1 half dc, 2 dc, sc in 3rd dc of corresponding shell on first block, and complete shell as before. Repeat from *** once more. In corner loop make: 1 sc, 1 half dc, 1 dc, sc in corresponding dc of corner shell on first block, and complete shell. Finish remainder of rnd as for first block.

THIRD BLOCK...Work exactly as for second block, joining on last rnd to one side of first block (adjacent to side joined before).

FOURTH BLOCK...Work as for second block, joining on last rnd to one side of third block, and the adjacent side of second block.

Make necessary number of blocks, joining each block on the last rnd as before.

Galaxy Bedspread

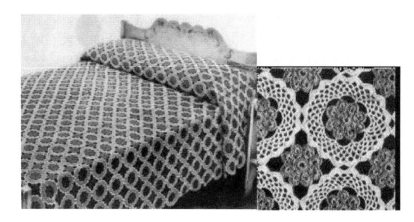

Galaxy Bedspread

Original Materials Knit-Cro-Sheen, 39 balls of a light color and 28 balls of a dark color for a double size spread; 31 balls of a light color and 24 balls of a dark color for a single size spread. (If desired, two shades of one color may be used.)

Suggested Materials - Crochet Thread Size 10 or 12 or size of your choice – Optional - Use a Crochet Cotton if Preferred for a heavier bedspread

Steel crochet hook No. 9.

GAUGE: Each large motif measures about 4 1/2 inches in diameter.

For a double size spread, 90 x 108 inches, make 20 x 24 motifs. For a single size spread, 72 x 108 inches, make 16 x 24 motifs.

FIRST MOTIF... Starting at center, with dark color ch 10 and join with sl st to form ring.

1st rnd: Ch 3 (to count as dc), 23 dc in ring. Join with sl st to 3rd st of ch-3 first made.

2nd rnd: Ch 3, dc in same place as sl st, ch 3, 2 dc in same place, * ch 1, skip 2 dc; in next dc make 2 dc, ch 3, 2 dc. Repeat from * around. Join last dc with sc to 3rd st of ch-3 first made (8 groups in all).

3rd rnd: * 9 dc in ch-3 sp, sc in ch-1 sp. Repeat from * around (8 shells). Fasten and break off.

4th rnd: Attach light color to center of next shell, * ch 11, sc in center dc of next shell. Repeat from * around. Join last ch-11 with sl st in center dc of 1st shell.

5th rnd: * Ch 4, skip 2 ch, sc in next st. Repeat from * around (32 ch-4 loops in all).

6th, 7th and 8th rnds: Sl st to center of next loop, * ch 4, sc in next loop. Repeat from * around. Join.

9th rnd: Sl st to center of next loop, sc in same loop, * 9 dc in next loop, sc in next loop. Repeat from * around. Join and break off.

SECOND MOTIF...Work as for first motif to 8th rnd incl.

9th rnd: Sl st to center of next loop, sc in same loop, 9 dc in next loop, sc in next loop, 4 dc in next loop, insert hook in 5th dc of a shell on first motif, 5 dc back in second motif (to complete shell), sc in next loop of same motif, 4 dc in next loop, insert hook in 5th dc of next shell on first motif, 5 dc back in second motif (to complete shell). Complete this rnd as for first motif, with no more joinings. Break off.

THIRD MOTIF...Join this motif to first motif in exactly the same way, leaving 2 shells free between motifs.

FOURTH MOTIF... Join this motif to second and third motifs in same way, leaving 2 shells free between motifs.

Make necessary number of motifs, joining each motif as before. Then make fill-in motifs in all spaces between joinings, as follows:

FILL-IN MOTIF...With dark color, work as for first 3 rnds of first motif, but on the 3rd rnd join to large motifs in same way as large motifs were joined.

Popcorn Star Bedspread 2

Popcorn Star Bedspread 2

Original Materials – Pearl Cottonvin size 3 with a No. 5 hook, or Pear Cotton in size 5 with a No. 6 hook or Crochet Cord with a No. 5 hook, may be used for making this six-pointed star spread with popcorns.

Suggested Materials - Crochet Thread Size 10 or 12 or size of your choice – Optional - Use a Crochet Cotton if Preferred for a heavier bedspread

The number of blocks needed for a spread will depend on the size of the finished block and the size desired for the completed spread.

Ch - chain

j - join

sk - skip

sl st - slip stitch

pc - popcorn

Ch 10, j for ring.

1st row: Ch 1, 24 sc in ring.

2nd row: *Ch 5, sk 1 st, sc in next st, repeat from * for 12 loops around ring.

3rd row: Sl st up 3 sts, *ch 3, sl st in 3rd ch of loop, repeat from *.

4th row: Ch 1, 6 sc over each ch 3.

5th row: S1 st 2 sts, ch 3, tr in same st with ch 3, ch 2, 2 tr in same st, *ch 1, sk 6 sts, 2 tr in next st, ch 2, 2 tr in same st, repeat from *.

6th row: Sl st to ch 2, ch 3, 6 tr over ch 2, *ch 1, 1 sc in ch, 1 sp, ch 1, 7 tr over next ch 2, repeat from * all around, j.

7th row: Ch 6, 1 sc in 4th st, *ch 3, tr in ch 1, ch 3, sk 3 sts, sc in next st, repeat from * all around, j.

8th row: Ch 5, 1 tr in same st, *(ch 2, sk 2, 1 tr in next st) 6 times, ch 2, 1 tr in same tr, repeat from * all around, j.

9th row: Sl st into ch 2, ch 5, *1 tr in same sp, (ch 2, 1 pc in next sp) 6 times, ch 2, 1 tr in next sp, ch 2, repeat from * all around, j, and sl into next sp.

To make the popcorn (pc) as indicated in this row, proceed as follows: Make 5 tr in one st. Remove and pass hook through the st of the first tr and the st of the last tr, and draw together. Make 1 ch st to hold it solid.

10th row: Ch 5, *1 tr in same sp, ch 2, 1 tr in next sp, (ch 2, 1 pc) 5 times, (ch 2, 1 tr in next sp) 2 times, ch 2, repeat from * all around hexagon, j.

11th row: Ch 5, *1 tr in same sp, (ch 2, 1 tr in next sp), 2 times, (ch 2, pc) 4 times, (ch 2, 1 tr in next sp) 3 times, ch 2, repeat from * around hexagon, j.

12th row: Ch 5, *1 tr in same sp, (ch 2, 1 tr in next sp) 3 times, (ch 2, 1 pc) 3 times, (ch 2, 1 tr in next sp) 4 times, ch 2, repeat from * all around hexagon, j.

13th row: Ch 5, *1 tr in same sp, (ch 2, 1 tr in next sp) 4 times, (ch 2, 1 pc) 2 times, (ch 2, 1 tr in next sp) 5 times, ch 2, repeat from * all around, j.

14th row: Ch 5, *1 tr in same sp, (ch 2, 1 tr in next sp) 5 times, ch 2, 1 pc, (ch 2, 1 tr in next sp) 6 times, ch 2, repeat from * all around, j.

15th row: Ch 5, * 1 tr in same sp, (ch 2, 1 tr in next sp) 13 times, ch 2, repeat from * all around, j.

16th row: Ch 5, *1 tr in same sp, (ch 2, 1 pc st in next sp, ch 2, tr in next sp) 7 times, ch 2, 1 tr in next sp, ch 2, repeat from * all around, j.

17th row: Ch 5, *1 tr in same sp, (ch 2, 1 tr in next sp) 15 times, ch 2, repeat from * all around, j.

18th row: Ch 5, * 1 tr in same sp, (ch 2, 1 pc in next sp, ch 2, tr in next sp) 8 times, ch 2, 1 tr in next sp, ch 2, repeat from *.

19th row: Ch 5, * 1 tr in same sp, (ch 2, 1 tr in next sp) 17 times, ch 2, repeat from * all around.

20th row: Ch 5, 1 tr in same sp, 1 tr in each st across each side of hexagon, with ch 2 in each corner, j.

21st row: Ch 5, 1 sc in same sp, *ch 5, sk 2 sts of last row, 1 sc in next st, repeat from * around hexagon, putting (2 sc with ch 5 between) in each corner.

Fringe: Cut cotton for fringe in 20-inch lengths. Take 6 of these and get the ends even, fold in center, slip this fold through an open space, and draw the 2 groups of ends through this fold and pull tightly. Repeat in every 2nd space. Take one-half of first group and one-half of 2nd group and loop in a knot one-half inch below the first knot of fringe. Repeat around the end and 2 sides. Next row: Take one-half of first group and one-half second group and tie in loop one-half inch below last row of knots. Repeat around. Make another row of knots as last row.

To Join Hexagons; Make the 21st row around one block. When this row is being made around the second block, begin to j at corner, ch 3, 1 sl st around corner loop of first bl, ch 3, sc in corner sp of second bl, *ch 3, 1 sl st around next loop of first bl, ch 3, sk 2 tr of second bl, 1 sc in next st, repeat from *.

Pineapple Frosting Bedspread

Pineapple Frosting Bedspread

Original Materials: Mercerized Bedspread Cotton

Suggested Materials - Crochet Thread Size 10 or 12 or preferred size – Optional - Use a Crochet Cotton if Preferred for a heavier bedspread

For Single Size Spread, 62 x 109 inches, 72 balls of No. 181 Shaded Lt. Yellows.

For Double Size Spread, 84 x 109 inches, 85 balls of No. 181 Shaded Lt. Yellows; or

For Single Size Spread, 62 x 109 inches, 72 balls of No. 9 Yellow.

For Double Size Spread, 84 x 109 inches, 85 balls of No. 9 Yellow.

Steel Crochet Hook No. 7.

GAUGE: Each block measures 11¼ inches from side to side.

FIRST BLOCK ... Starting at center, ch 10. Join with sl st to form ring.

1st rnd: Ch 3, 23 dc in ring. Join with sl st to top of ch-3.

2nd rnd: Sc in same place as sl st, * ch 3, skip 1 dc, sc in next dc. Repeat from * around. Join.

3rd rnd: Sl st in next loop, ch 3, 4 dc in same loop, drop loop from hook, insert hook in top of ch-3, draw dropped loop through (pc st made), * ch 5, 5 dc in next loop, drop loop from hook, insert hook in first dc, draw dropped loop through (another pc st made). Repeat from * around. Join.

4th rnd: Sl st in next sp, ch 3, 4 dc in same sp, * ch 3, 5 dc in next sp. Repeat from * around. Join.

5th rnd: Ch 4, holding back on hook the last loop of each tr make tr in next 4 dc, thread over and draw through all loops on hook (cluster made), * ch 5, dc in next sp, ch 5, cluster over next 5 dc. Repeat from * around. Join to tip of first cluster.

6th rnd: Sl st in next loop, sc in same loop, (ch 5, sc in next loop) twice; * ch 7, sc in next loop, (ch 5, sc in next loop) 3 times. Repeat from * around, ending with ch 2, dc in first sc.

7th rnd: * (Ch 5, sc in next loop) twice; 15 dc in next loop, sc in next loop. Repeat from * around. Join. 8th rnd: Sl st to center of next loop, sc in same loop, * ch 5, sc in next loop, (dc in next dc, ch 1) 14 times; dc in next dc, sc in next loop. Repeat from * around. Join.

9th rnd: Sl st to center of next loop, sc in same loop, * ch 4, (sc in next ch.1 sp, ch 3) 13 times; sc in next sp, ch 4, sc in next loop. Repeat from * around. Join.

10th rnd: Sc in same place as sl st, * sc in next loop, ch 1, (pc st in next loop, ch 2) 12 times; pc st in next loop, ch 1, sc in next loop, sc in next sc. Repeat from * around. Join.

11th rnd: Sl st to first ch-2 sp, sc in same sp * (ch 3, sc in next sp) 11 times; ch 2, skip next sc, in next sc make 2 dc, ch 2 and 2 dc (shell made); ch 2, sc in next ch-2 sp. Repeat from * around. Join.

12th rnd: Sl st in next loop, ch 3, pc st in same loop, * (ch 2, pc st in next loop) 10 times; ch 4, in sp of next shell make (2 dc, ch 2) twice and 2 dc; ch 4, pc st in next ch-3 loop. Repeat from * around. Join. 13th rnd: Sl st in next sp, sc in next sp, * (ch 3, sc in next sp) 9 times; ch 4, skip next sp, shell in next sp, ch 2, shell in next sp, ch 4, skip next sp, sc in next sp. Repeat from * around. Join.

14th rnd: Sl st in next loop, ch 3, pc st in the same loop, * (ch 2, pc st in next loop) 8 times; ch 4, shell in sp of next shell (shell made over shell), ch 5, sc in next sp, ch 5, shell over next shell, ch 4, skip next sp, pc st in next loop. Repeat from * around. Join.

15th rnd: Sl st in next sp, sc in same sp, * (ch 3, sc in next sp) 7 times; ch 4, shell over shell, ch 5, 2 sc in next sp, sc in next sc, 2 sc in next sp, ch 5, shell over next shell, ch 4, skip next sp, sc in next sp. Repeat from * around. Join.

16th rnd: Sl st in next loop, ch 3, pc st in same loop, * (ch 2, pc st in next loop) 6 times; ch 4, shell over shell, ch 5, 2 sc in next loop, sc in next 5 sc, 2 sc in next loop ch 5 shell over shell, ch 4, skip next sp, pc st in next loop. Repeat from * around Join

17th rnd: Sl st in next sp, sc in same sp, * (ch 3, sc in next sp) 5 times, ch 4, shell over shell, ch 5, 2 sc in next sp, sc in next 9 sc, 2 sc in next sp, ch 5, shell over shell, ch 4, skip next sp, sc in next sp. Repeat from * around. Join.

18th rnd: Sl st in next loop, ch 3, pc st in same loop, * (ch 2, pc st in next loop) 4 times; ch 4, shell over shell, ch 5, 2 sc in next sp, sc in each sc across, 2 sc in next sp, ch 5, shell over shell, ch 4, skip next sp, pc st in next loop. Repeat from * around. Join.

19th rnd: Sl st in next sp, sc in same sp, * (ch 3, sc in next sp) 3 times; ch 4, shell over shell, ch 5, 2 sc in next loop, sc in each sc across, 2 sc in next loop, ch 5, shell over shell, ch 4, skip next sp, sc in next loop. Repeat from * around. Join.

20th rnd: Sl st in next loop, ch 3, pc st in same loop, * (ch 2, pc st in next sp) twice; ch 4, shell over shell, ch 5, 2 sc in next sp, sc in each sc across, 2 sc in next sp, ch 5, shell over shell, ch 4, skip next sp, pc st in next loop. Repeat from * around. Join.

21st rnd: Sl st in next sp, sc in same sp, *S ch 3, sc in next sp, ch 4, shell over shell, ch 5, 2 sc in next sp, ch 5, skip 4 sc, sc in next sc, ch 5, skip 4 sc, sc in next 7 sc, ch 5, skip 4 sc, sc in next sc, ch 5, 2 sc in next sp, ch 5, shell over shell, ch 4, skip next sp, sc in next sp. Repeat from * around. Join.

22nd rnd: Sl st in next loop, ch 3, pc st in same loop, * ch 4, shell over shell, (ch 5, 2 sc in next loop) 3 times; ch 5, skip 3 sc, sc in next sc, (Ch 5, 2 sc in next loop) 3 times; Ch 5, shell over shell, Ch 4, skip next sp, pc st in next loop. Repeat from * around. Join.

23rd rnd: Sl st to sp of next shell, ch 3, in same sp make dc, ch 2 and 2 dc; * (ch 5, 2 sc in next loop) 8 times; ch 5, shell over next 2 shells. Repeat from * around. Join and break off.

SECOND BLOCK... Work as for First Block until 22 rnds have been completed.

23rd rnd: Sl st to sp of next shell, ch 3, dc in same sp, ch 1, sl st in sp of corresponding shell on First Block, ch 1, 2 dc in same sp on Second Block, (ch 2, sl st in next loop on First Block, ch 2, 2 sc in next loop on Second Block) 8 times; ch 2, sl st in next loop on First Block, ch 2, 2 dc in sp of next shell on Second Block, ch 1, sl st in sp of corresponding shell on First Block ch 1 2 dc in sp of same shell on Second Block. Complete rnd (no more joinings).

For Single Size Spread, make 6 rows of 5 blocks and 5 rows of 4 blocks. For Double Size Spread, make 6 rows of 7 blocks and 5 rows of 6 blocks. Join as in diagram.

HALF BLOCK Starting at center, ch 10. Join with sl st to form ring.

1st row: Ch 3, 14 dc in ring. Ch 1, turn.

2nd row: Sc in first dc, * ch 3, skip l dc, sc in next dc. Repeat from * across, ending with sc in top of turning chain. Ch 5, turn.

3rd row: Pc st in first loop, * ch 5, pc st in next loop, repeat from across, ending with ch 2, dc in last sc. Ch 6, turn.

4th row: Skip first sp, (5 dc in next sp, ch 3) 6 times; skip 2 ch of turning chain, dc in next ch. Ch 8, turn. 5th row: Skip first dc, * tr cluster over next 5 dc, ch 5, dc in next sp, ch 5. Repeat from * across, ending with dc in 3rd ch of turning chain. Ch lt), turn.

6th row: Sc in first loop, * (ch 5, sc in next loop) 3 times; ch 7, sc in next loop. Repeat from * once more, (ch 5, sc in next loop) 3 times; ch 7, dc in same loop as last sc was made. Ch 3, turn.

7th row: 8 dc in the first loop, * (sc in next loop, ch 5) twice; sc in next loop, 15 dc in next loop. Repeat from * once more, (sc in next loop, ch 5) twice; sc in next loop, 9 dc in next loop. Ch 4, turn.

8th row: Skip first dc, (dc in next dc, ch 1) 7 times; dc in next dc, sc in next loop, ch 5, sc in next loop, (dc in next dc, ch 1) 14 times; dc in next dc. Repeat from * once more, sc in next loop, ch 5, sc in next loop, (dc in next dc, ch 1) 8 times; dc in top of turning chain. Ch 1, turn.

9th row: Sc in first dc, ch 3, skip next sp, (sc in next sp, ch 3) 6 times; sc in next sp, * ch 4, sc in next loop, ch 4, (sc in next sp, ch 3) 13 times; sc in next sp. Repeat from * once more, ch 4, sc in next loop, ch 5, (sc in next sp, ch 3) 7 times; sc in 3rd ch of turning chain. Ch 4. turn.

10th row: Pc st in first loop, (ch 2, pc st in next loop) 6 times; * ch 1, sc in next loop, sc in next sc, sc in next loop, ch 1, (pc st in next loop, ch 2) 12 times; pc st in next loop. Repeat from * once more, ch 1, sc in next loop, sc in next sc, sc in next loop, ch 1, (pc st in next loop, ch 2) 6 times; pc st in next loop, ch 1, dc in next sc. Ch 1, turn.

11th row: Sc in first dc, (ch 3, sc in next ch-2 sp) 6 times; * ch 2, skip 1 sc, shell in next sc, ch 2, (sc in next ch 2 sp, ch 3) 11 times; sc in next sp. Repeat from * once more, skip 1 sc, shell in next sc, ch 2, (sc in next ch-2 sp, ch 3) 6 times; sc in 3rd ch of turning chain. Ch 4, turn.

12th row: Pc st in first loop, (ch 2, pc st in next loop) 5 times; * ch 4, in sp of next shell make (2 dc, ch 2) twice and 2 dc; ch 4, (pc st in next ch-3 loop, ch 2) 10 times; pc st in next loop. Repeat from * once more, ch 4, in sp of next shell make (2 dc, ch 2) twice and 2 dc; ch 4, (pc st in next ch-3 loop, ch 2) 5 times; pc st in next loop, ch 1, dc in last sc. Ch 1, turn.

Continue to work as for Block, keeping each side straight and having 1 pc st less on inside edge of each end pineapple, until 1 pc st remains.

Next row: Work as for last row of Block, joining adjacent sides to free sides of 1st, 2nd and 3rd rows of completed blocks. Make necessary number of half blocks to even off long sides and join as before.

RUFFLE

1st row: Leaving 2 sides free on end motif, attach thread between next 2 shells. Working across long side, ch 5, in sp between shells make sc, ch 5 and sc; * (ch 5, sc in next loop) 5 times; ch 5, in next loop make sc, ch 5 and sc (1 loop increased). Repeat from * around 3 sides. Ch 5, turn.

2nd and 3rd rows: * Sc in next loop, ch 5. Repeat from * around. Ch 5, turn.

4th row: * (Sc in next loop, ch 5) 6 times; inc 1 loop. Repeat from * around. Ch 5, turn.

5th, 6th and 7th rows: Repeat 2nd, 3rd and 4th rows, having 1 loop more between increases on 7th row.

8th and 9th rows: Repeat 2nd row. Break off at end of 9th row.

Block to measurements.

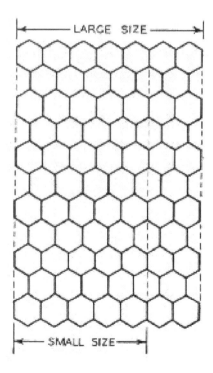

Heavenly Daydream Bedspread

Heavenly Daydream Bedspread

Original Materials: SIX CORD MERCERIZED CROCHET, Size 20: Single size 133 balls, Double Size 168 Balls.

Steel Crochet Hook No. 8 or 9.

Suggested Materials - Crochet Thread Size 10 or 12 or preferred size – Optional - Use a Crochet Cotton if Preferred for a heavier bedspread

GAUGE: Each motif measures about 6 1/4 inches in diameter.

For single size spread about 74 x 108 inches, make 11 x 16 motifs; for double size spread about 94 x 108 inches, make 14 x 16 motifs.

FIRST MOTIF . . . Ch 9, join with sl st to form ring. 1st rnd: (Ch 7, 4 sc in ring) 4 times. Do not join rnds.

2nd rnd: (Ch 7, 4 sc in next loop, sc in next 2 sc) 4 times.

3rd to 19th rnds incl: (Ch 7, 4 sc in next loop, sc in each sc across to last 2 sc of this group, do not work in these last 2 sc) 4 times. There are 40 sc in each group on 19th rnd.

20th rnd: * Ch 7, sc in next loop, (ch 7, skip 3 sc, sc in next sc) 9 times. Repeat from * 3 more times (40 loops).

21st rnd: * Ch 7, sc in next loop. Repeat from * around.

22nd and 23rd rnds: * Ch 8, sc in next loop. Repeat from * around, ch 4, tr in 1st loop of 23rd rnd.

24th rnd: Ch 1, sc in tr, * in next loop make 4 tr, ch 3 and 4 tr, sc in next loop. Repeat from * around. Join last tr with sl st in 1st sc.

25th rnd: * Ch 5, in next sp make tr, ch 3, sc in 3rd ch from hook (p made), (tr, p) 3 times, and tr, ch 5, sc in next sc. Repeat from * around. Join, fasten off.

SECOND MOTIF . . . Work as for 1st Motif until 24th rnd is completed.

25th rnd: * Ch 5, in next sp make tr, p, (tr, ch 1, sc in corresponding p on 1st Motif, ch 1) twice, complete the picot on 2nd Motif; tr, p and tr, ch 5, sc in next sc. Repeat from * 2 more times (3 joinings). Complete rnd as for 1st Motif.

Make necessary number of motifs, joining to adjacent sides as 2nd Motif was joined to 1st, leaving 2 groups free between joinings.

FILL-IN MOTIF ... Ch 8, join with sl st to form ring.

1st rnd: Ch 3 (to count as dc), 23 dc in ring. Join with sl st in 3rd st of ch-3.

2nd rnd: * Ch 13, sl st in 6th ch from hook, ch 5, skip 2 dc, sl st in next dc. Repeat from * around. Join last ch-5 with sl st in base of first ch-13.

3rd rnd: Sl st in 6 ch, sl st in large loop, ch 3, 12 dc in small loop, * 13 dc in next small loop. Repeat from * around. Join.

4th rnd: * Ch 8, sl st between center p's of group (before the joining) between motifs, ch 7, sl st in center dc of next shell, ch 13, sl st in next joining of motifs, ch 13, sl st in center dc of next shell, ch 7, sl st between p's of next free group, ch 8, sc between shells. Repeat from * around. Join and fasten off. Fill in all sps between motifs in this manner.

Royal Society Filet Bedspread

Royal Society Filet Bedspread

Original Materials – EVERSHEEN

Single Size Spread: 68 x 108 inches - 30 balls

Double Size Spread: 90 x 108 inches - 45 balls.

OR

CROCHET and KNITTING COTTON - 600 yard hanks

Single Size Spread: 68 x 108 inches -15 hanks.

Double Size Spread: 90 x 108 inches - 23 hanks,

Steel Crochet Hook, No. 7.

Suggested Materials - Crochet Thread Size 10 or 12 or Preferred size – Optional - Use a Crochet Cotton if Preferred for a heavier bedspread

GAUGE: 3 sps make 1 inch; 3 rows make 1 inch.

STRIP . . . Ch 102

1st row: Sc in 10th ch from hook, ch 3, skip 2 ch, dc in next ch (lacet made), ch 3, skip 2 ch, sc in next ch, ch 3, skip 2 ch, dc in next ch (another lacet made); make 3 more lacets, dc in next 6 ch (2 bls made); ch 2, skip 2 ch, dc in next ch (sp made), make 2 more sps, dc in next 3 dc (bl made), (3 sps, 1 bl) twice; 2 sps, 2 bls, 2 lacets. Ch 8, turn.

2nd row: Dc in next dc (bar made), ch 5, dc in next dc (another bar made), dc in next 6 dc (2 bls made over 2 bls), ch 2, dc in next dc (sp made over sp), 1 more sp, ch 2, skip 2 dc, dc in next dc (sp made over bl). 2 dc in next sp, dc in next dc (bl made over sp), (3 sps, 1 bl) twice; 2 sps, 2 bls, 4 bars, ch 5, dc in 4th ch of turning chain. Ch 6, turn.

3rd row: Sc in center ch of bar, ch 3, dc in next dc (lacet made over bar), make 4 more lacets, ch 3, skip 2 dc, sc in next dc, ch 3, skip 2 dc, dc in next dc (lacet made over 2 bls), 2 bls, (3 sps, 1 bl) 3 times; 2 sps, 5 dc under bar, dc in next dc (2 bls made over bar), ch 3, skip 2 ch, sc in next ch, ch 3, skip 2 ch, dc in next ch. Ch 8, turn.

4th row: 1 bar, 2 bls, (3 sps, 1 bl) 3 times; 2 sps, 2 bls; 6 bars. Ch 6, turn.

5th row: 7 lacets, 2 bls, (3 sps, 1 bl) 3 times; 2 sps, 2 bls. Ch 3, turn.

6th row: 2 bls, (3 sps, 1 bl) 3 times; 2 sps, 2 bls, 7 bars. Ch 6, turn.

7th row: 8 lacets, 2 bls, (3 sps, 1 bl) 3 times; 2 sps. Ch 5, turn.

8th row: (3 sps, 1 bl) 3 times; 2 sps, 2 bls, 8 bars. Ch 6, turn.

Starting at the 9th row, follow chart to top (this completes one pattern). Make 4 more patterns and break off.

For Single Size Spread, make 6 strips. For Double Size Spread, make 8 strips. Sew strips neatly together, having corresponding parts of design meet (see picture).

EDGING . . . Attach thread to a sp, sc in same sp, ch 3, sl st in last sc (picot made), sc in same sp. In each sp or bl around make sc, picot and sc. Join and break off.

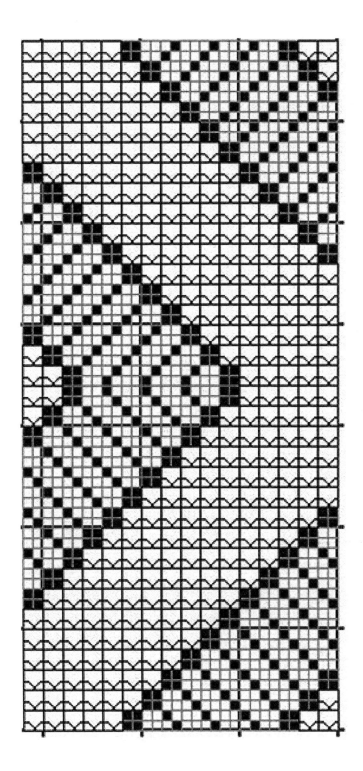

The Puritan Bedspread

The Puritan Bedspred – Star Book 126

Original Materials: Mercerized Crochet Cotton

Suggested Materials - Crochet Thread Size 10 or 12 or size of your choice – Optional - Use a Crochet Cotton if Preferred for a heavier bedspread

52 balls White, Cream or Ecru.

Steel crochet hook No. 7.

Each Motif measures about 5 inches. 216 Motifs (12 x 18) are required to make spread measuring about 62 inches x 92 inches without the 7inch fringe.

Ch 6, join to form a ring.

2nd Row: Ch 6, d c in ring, * ch 3, d c in same ring, repeat from * 5 times, ch 3, join in 3rd st of ch.

3rd Row: Ch 1, 2 sc in 1st mesh, ** ch 14, d c in 6th st from hook, * ch 2, skip 2 sts of ch, d c in next st, repeat from * once, ch 1, turn.

4th Row: 1 sc in d c, 2 sc in next mesh, 1 sc in next d c, 2 sc in next mesh, 1 sc in next d c, 1 sc in each of the next 2 sts of ch, 3 sc in next st of ch, 1 sc in each of the next 2 sts of ch, 1 sc in next d c, 2 sc in next mesh, 1 sc in next d c, 2 sc in next mesh, 1 sc in last d c, ch 1, turn.

5th Row: 1 sc in each of the next 10 sc picking up the back loop of sts only, 3 sc in next st, 1 sc in each of the next 10 sc, ch 1, turn.

6th Row: 1 sc in each of the next 11 sc picking up the back loop of sts only, 3 sc in next st, 1 sc in each of the next 11 sc, ** ch 1, turn.

7th Row: 1 sc in each of the next 12 sc picking up the back loop of sts only, 3 sc in next st, 1 sc in each of the next 12 sc. With right side of work toward you, sl loop off hook, fold the petal through the center lengthwise, insert hook in 1st st of 7th row, pick up loop and sl st across lower edge and the 2 remaining chs of stem, flatten out petal again, work 2 sc over remainder of 1st mesh, ch 5, sl st in 5th st from hook for picot, 2 sc in next mesh and repeat between ** of 3rd and 6th rows, ch 1, turn.

8th Row: 1 sc in each of the 1st 3 sc picking up back loop of sts only, slip loop off hook, insert hook in back loop of corresponding st of previous petal made and pull through loop to join, 1 sc in each of the next 3 sc, join to corresponding st of previous petal, 1 sc in each of the next 6 sc, 3 sc in next st, 1 sc in each of the next 12 sc, complete petal same as previous petal and continue until there are 8 petals joining the last petal to 1st petal made, cut thread.

9th Row: Join thread in point of petal, ch 6, d c in same space, * ch 2, skip 1 st, d c in next st, ch 2, skip 1 st, d c in next st, ch 2, skip 1 st, tr c in next st, skip 1st free st on next petal, tr c in next st, ch 2, skip 1 st, d c in next st, ch 2, skip 1 st, d c in next st, ch 2, skip 1 st, d c in point of petal, ch 3, d c in same space, repeat from * all around, ch 2, join in 3rd st of ch.

10th Row: Ch 1, * 3 sc in 1st mesh, 1 sc in next d c, 2 sc in next mesh, sc in next d c, 2 sc in next mesh, sc in next d c, 2 sc in next mesh, skip next 2 tr c, 2 sc in each of the next 3 meshes, 1 sc in each of the next 3 d c, repeat from * all around.

11th Row: Ch 5, skip 3 sc, 1 sc in each of the next 7 sc, ch 3, skip 4 sc, 1 sc in each of the next 17 sc, ch 3, skip 4 sc, 1 sc in each of the next 7 sc, repeat from beginning all around.

12th Row: Sl st into loop, ch 6, tr c in same loop, * ch 1, tr c in same loop, repeat from * 4 times, ** ch 3, skip 1 sc, 1 sc in each of the next 5 sc, ch 4, skip 1 sc of next group of sc, 1 sc in each of the next 15 sc, ch 4, skip 1 sc of next group of sc, 1 sc in each of the next 5 sc, ch 3, 1 tr c in next loop, * ch 1, tr c in same loop, repeat from * 5 times, repeat from ** all around, ch 3, join in 5th st of ch.

13th Row: Sc in next loop, * ch 3, sc in next loop, repeat from * 5 times, ** ch 3, skip 1 sc, 1 sc in each of the next 3 sc, ch 3, d c in next loop, ch 3, skip 1 sc, 1 sc in each of the next 13 sc, ch 3, d c in next loop, ch 3, skip 1 sc, 1 sc in each of the next 3 sc, * ch 3, sc in next loop, repeat from * 7 times, repeat from ** all around completing the loops at corner.

14th Row: Sl st to next loop, ch 2, sc in next loop, ch 2, sc in next loop, ch 3, sc in same loop (this is the corner), * ch 2, sc in next loop, repeat from * 3 times, * ch 2, d c in next loop, repeat from * once, ch 2, skip 2 sc, 1 sc in each of the next 9 sc, * ch 2, d c in next loop, repeat from * once, * ch 2, sc in next loop, repeat from * 4 times, ch 3, sc in same loop, * ch 2, sc in next loop, repeat from * 3 times, continue around in same manner.

15th Row: Ch 1, 2 sc in each of the next 2 loops, 5 sc in corner loop, 2 sc in each of the next 4 loops, 3 sc in each of the next 3 loops, skip 1 sc, 1 sc in each of the next 7 sc, continue all around in same manner.

16th Row: Working in back loop of sts only, work 1 sc in each sc working 3 sc in each corner, cut thread.

Work 215 more motifs in same manner. Sew motifs together.

EDGE: Attach thread in corner and working across top, ch 4, d c in same space, * ch 1, skip 1 st, d c in next st, repeat from * all around working 1 d c, ch 1, 1 d c in center st at each corner, join.

2nd Row: * Ch 3, 2 d c in same space, skip one mesh, sl st in next mesh, ch 3, 2 d c in same space, skip 1 d c and 1 mesh, sl st in next d c, repeat from * across top edge only, cut thread.

FRINGE: Wind thread over a 7 inch cardboard. Cut one end.

Using 14 strands, double in half and loop through every other mesh on the 3 sides. * Take half of one group of fringe and half of next group of fringe, knot together about 1/2 inch from 1st row of knots, repeat from * all around. Trim fringe evenly.

Irish Crochet Bedspread 2

Irish Crochet Bedspread 2

Materials: Six Cord Mercerized Crochet Cord, Size 20:

Big Ball: 70 balls for Single Size: 86 balls for Double Size; Steel Crochet Hook No. 8 or 9.

Suggested Materials - Crochet Thread Size 10 or 12 or size of your choice – Optional - Use a Crochet Cotton if Preferred for a heavier bedspread

Motif measures 3 1/4 inches in diameter after blocking.

For a single size spread 72 x 105 inches, make 22 x 32 motifs.

For a double size spread about 88 x 105 inches, make 27 x 32 motifs.

MOTIF . . . Ch 10. Join with sl st.

1st rnd: Ch 1, 18 sc in ring. Sl st in 1st sc made.

2nd rnd: Ch 1, sc in same place as sl st, * ch 5, skip 2 sc, sc in next sc. Repeat from * 5 more times; ch 5, join with sl st in 1st sc.

3rd rnd: Ch 1, in each loop around make sc, half dc, 5 dc, half dc and sc (6 petals). Join.

4th rnd: Ch 1, sc in same place as sl st, * ch 7, insert hook in next loop from back to front of work, bring it out in next loop from front to back of work; thread over, draw loop through, thread over and draw through all loops on hook. Repeat from * around. Join (6 loops).

5th rnd: In each loop around make sc, half dc, dc, 7 tr, dc, half dc and sc (6 petals).

6th rnd: Repeat 4th rnd.

7th rnd: Sl st in 1st loop, ch 3, 7 dc in same loop, 8 dc in each loop around (48 dc on rnd). Join with sl st in 3rd st of ch-3.

8th rnd: Ch 3, dc in next 2 dc, * ch 2, dc in next 3 dc, ch 4, sc in 4th ch from hook (p made), dc in next 3 dc. Repeat from * around. Join.

9th rnd: Ch 3, dc in next 2 dc, * ch 2, dc in next 3 dc, ch 1, p, ch 1, dc in next 3 dc. Repeat from * around. Join.

10th rnd: Ch 3, dc in next 2 dc, * ch 2, dc in next 3 dc, ch 2, p, ch 2, dc in next 3 dc. Repeat from * around. Join.

11th rnd: Ch 3, dc in next 2 dc, * ch 2, dc in next 3 dc, ch 11, dc in next 3 dc. Repeat from * around. Join.

12th rnd: Ch 3, dc in next 2 dc, * ch 2, dc in next 3 dc, 11 dc in next sp, dc in next 3 dc. Repeat from * around. Join and break off.

Make necessary number of motifs and sew corresponding (9 dc, ch 2 and 9 dc) sides of adjacent motifs together with neat over-and-over sts on wrong side. There will be one group of 8 dc, ch 2 and 8 dc free between joinings.

FILL-IN-MOTIF . . . Ch 7, join with sl st.

1st rnd: Ch 3, 15 dc in ring. Join with sl st to top st of ch-3.

2nd rnd: Ch 7, * skip 1 dc, dc in next dc, ch 4. Repeat from * around, joining last ch-4 with sl st in 3rd st of ch-7 (8 sps).

3rd rnd: Sl st in sp, ch 3, 7 dc in same sp, 8 dc in each following sp around. Join and break off.

Sew 8 dc of Fill-in-motif to center 3 dc, ch 2 and 3 dc of free group on large motif. Sew 3 adjacent groups in this manner, leaving 4 groups of 8 dc free on Fill-in-motif. Fill in all sps between motifs in same way.

Popcorn Bedspread 2

Popcorn Bedspread 2

Original Materials: Cro-Sheen 74 balls for Single Size; 90 balls for Double Size

Suggested Materials - Crochet Thread Size 10 or 12 or size of your choice – Optional - Use a Crochet Cotton if Preferred for a heavier bedspread

Steel Crochet Hook No. 7.

Each block measures about 5 inches square.

Done in WW Yarn with an H or I hook (depending how tight you crochet) square will equal 12 inches

For a single size spread 72 x 108 inches, including fringe, make 13 x 20 blocks. For a double size spread, 90 x 108 inches, including fringe, make 16 x 20 blocks.

Comfortghan size - 3 x 4 blocks - 36 inches x 48

BLOCK . . . Starting at center, ch 10. join with sl st. *(I used ch 6 when working with yarn)*

1st rnd: Ch 3 (to count as dc), * make a pc st in ring - *to make a pc st, ch 1, make 5 dc in ring, drop loop from hook, insert hook in ch-1 preceding 5 dc and draw dropped loop through; make dc in ring.* Repeat from * until 8 pc sts are complete. Join to top of ch 3.

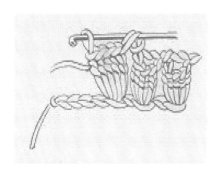

2nd rnd: Ch 3 (to count as 1 dc), holding back on hook the last loop of next 2 dc, make 2 dc in same place as sl st, thread over and draw through all loops on hook (a 3-dc cluster made); ch 3, holding back on hook the last loop of next 3 dc make 3 dc in same place as last cluster; thread over and draw through all loops on hook (another 3-dc cluster made). * Ch 2 skip next pc st, 3 dc in next dc, ch 2, skip next pc st, in next dc make a cluster, ch 3 and a cluster. Repeat from * around. Join last ch-2 to top of lst cluster.

3rd rnd: Sl st in next sp, ch 3 (to count as dc), in same sp make cluster, ch 3 and cluster, * ch 2, 2 dc in next sp, dc in next 3 dc, 2 dc in next sp, ch 2, in next sp (corner sp) make cluster, ch 3 and cluster. Repeat from * around. Join last ch-2 to top of lst cluster.

4th rnd: Sl st in next sp, ch 3 (to count as dc), in same sp make cluster, ch 3 and cluster. * ch 2, 2 dc in next sp, dc in next 7 dc, 2 dc in next sp, ch 2, in corner sp make cluster, ch 3 and cluster. Repeat from * around. Join last ch-2 to 1st cluster.

5th rnd: Sl st in next sp, ch 3 (to count as dc), in same sp make cluster, ch 3 and cluster, * ch 2, 2 dc in next sp, dc in next 5 dc, pc st in next dc, dc in next 5 dc, 2 dc in next sp, ch 2; in corner sp make cluster, ch-3 and cluster. Repeat from * around. Join.

6th rnd: Sl st in next sp, ch 3 (to count as dc), in same sp make cluster, ch 3 and cluster. * Ch 2, 2 dc in next sp, dc in next 5 dc, pc st in next dc, dc in next dc, dc back of next pc st and in following dc, pc st in next dc, dc in next 5 dc, 2 dc in next sp, ch 2; in corner sp make cluster, ch 3 and cluster. Repeat from * around. Join.

7th rnd: Sl st in next sp, ch 3, in same sp make cluster, ch 3 and cluster. * Ch 2, 2 dc in next sp, dc in next 5 dc, pc st in next dc, (dc in next dc, dc in back of pc st and in following dc, pc st in next dc) twice; dc in next 5 dc, 2 dc in next sp, ch 2; in corner sp make cluster, ch 3 and cluster. Repeat from * around. Join.

8th rnd: Sl st in next sp, ch 3, in same sp make cluster, ch 3 and cluster, * ch 2, 2 dc in next sp, dc in next 5 dc, pc st in next dc, (dc in next dc, dc in back of pc st, dc in next dc, pc st in next dc) 3 times; dc in next 5 dc, 2 dc in next sp; in corner sp make cluster, ch 3 and cluster. Repeat from * around. Join.

9th rnd: Sl st in next sp, ch 3, in same sp make cluster, ch 3 and cluster; * ch 2, 2 dc in next sp, dc in next 5 dc, pc st in next dc, (dc in next dc, dc in back of pc st, dc in next dc, pc st in next dc) 4 times; dc in next 5 dc, 2 dc in next ch 2, in corner sp make cluster, ch 3 cluster. Repeat from * around. Join and break off.

Make the necessary number of blocks and sew together neatly with over-and-over sts on wrong side.

FRINGE *(I'm omitting fringe for comfortghan)*

Work a row of ch-2 sps (ch 2 and dc) along two long sides and one short side. Then make fringe in each sp along these 3 sides as follows: Cut 8 strands, each 12 inches long. Double these strands, forming a loop. Pull loop through a sp, then draw loose ends through loop. Pull tight. Trim fringe evenly to 4 inches. Block bedspread to measurements given.

Pic of block worked in WW yarn

Texas Bedspread

Texas Bedspread

Original Materials Coats Knit Cro Sheen

Single Size Spread-70 x 120 inches-45 balls of No. 1 White and 31 balls of No. 131 Fudge Brown.

Double Size Spread-90 x 120 inches-56 balls of No. 1 White and 40 balls of No. 131 Fudge Brown; or

Mercerized Bedspread Cotton

Single Size Spread-70 x 120 inches-45 balls of No. 1 White and 31 balls of a color of your own choice.

Double Size Spread-90 x 120 inches-56 balls of No. 1 White and 40 balls of a color of your own choice; or

Bedspread Cotton

Single Size Spread-70 x 120 inches-55 balls of No. I White or No. 61 Ecru.

Double Size Spread-90 x 120 inches-70 balls of No. 1 White or No. 61 Ecru.

Steel Crochet Hook No. 7

Suggested Materials - Crochet Thread Size 10 or 12 or size of your choice – Optional - Use a Crochet Cotton if Preferred for a heavier bedspread

GAUGE: Each motif measures 6 inches from point to point

MOTIF . . . Starting at center with White, ch 8. Join with sl st to form ring.

1st rnd: 18 sc in ring. Join to first sc.

2nd rnd: Sc in same place as sl st, * ch 5. skip 2 sc, sc in next sc. Repeat from * around. Join.

3rd rnd: Sl st in next loop, ch 5, 7 d tr in same loop, make 8 d tr in each loop around. Join to top of ch-5.

4th rnd: Picking up back loop only, make sc in same place as sl st, sc in next 7 d tr, * ch 3, sc in next 8 d tr. Repeat from * around. Join and break off.

5th rnd: Attach Fudge Brown to any loop, ch 4, holding back on hook the last loop of each tr make 2 tr in same loop, thread over and draw through all loops on hook (cluster made), ch 5, make a 3-tr cluster in same loop, * (ch 3, skip 2 sc, cluster in next sc) twice; ch 3, in next loop make cluster, ch 5 and cluster. Repeat from * around. Join and break off.

6th rnd: Attach White to any ch-5 sp, in same sp make 3 sc, ch 3 and 3 sc; * 3 sc in each of next 3 sps, in next sp make 3 sc, ch 3 and 3 sc. Repeat from * around. Join.

7th rnd: Sl st in next 2 sc, ch 4, 2-tr cluster in same sc, * ch 3, in next loop make cluster, ch 5 and cluster; (ch 3, skip 2 sc, cluster in next sc) 5 times. Repeat from * around. Join.

8th rnd: Sl st in next sp, 3 sc in same sp, * in next sp make 3 sc, ch 3 and 3 sc; make 3 sc in each of next 6 sps. Repeat from * around. Join and break off.

9th rnd: Attach Brown to any sc, sc in each sc around, making 5 sc in each ch-3 loop. Join and break off. Attach Brown to free loop of any d tr on 3rd rnd sc in each loop around. Join and break off.

For Single Size Spread, make 8 rows of 24 motifs and 7 rows of 23 motifs. For Double Size Spread, make 10 rows of 24 motifs and 9 rows of 23 motifs.

To Join Motifs: With wrong sides facing and working through both thicknesses, attach Brown to back loop of center sc of any 5-sc group, sc in back loop of each sc across to center sc of next 5-sc group. Break off.

Join all motifs in this manner, following diagram. Block to measurements.

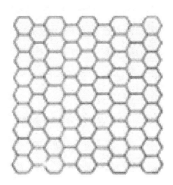

TASSEL . . . Cut 50 strands of White, each 12 inches long. Fold these strands and tie a separate piece of thread securely at top. Cut another piece 18 inches long and wind tightly around Tassel, 1 inch from top. Fasten ends securely. Make necessary number of Tassels and sew in place as illustrated.

Wakefield Bedspread

Wakefield Bedspread

Original Materials - MINERVA MELLOSHEEN

White No. 1930 - 17 Skeins

or

MINERVA CHALIMAR

White No. 1900 - 15 Skeins

Suggested Materials - Crochet Thread Size 10 or 12 or size of your choice – Optional - Use a Crochet Cotton if Preferred for a heavier bedspread

This amount is sufficient for a single size spread.

1 No. 9 Steel Crochet Hook

Scale: 1 motif about 4 inches square

The bedspread is 18 motifs wide and 25 motifs long (about 72" x 100").

MOTIF: Ch. 10, join in a ring.

Row 1: Ch. 3, work 31 DC. in ring. Join with a slip st. in 3rd Ch. of Ch. 3.

Row 2: Ch. 8, skip 3 DC., 1 DC. in. next DC, * Ch. 5, skip 3 DC., 1 DC. in next DC., repeat from * around row, ending Ch. 5, 1 slip st. in 3rd Ch. of Ch. 8 (8 spaces).

Row 3: Ch. 2, 7 SC. in each space, ending with a slip st. in second Ch. of Ch. 2.

Row 4: Ch. 5, 1 DC. in each of the first 2 SC., 2 DC. in each of the next 2 SC., 1 DC. in each of the next 3 SC. (9 DC.), * Ch. 3, 1 DC. in next SC., Ch. 10, skip 5 SC., 1 DC. in next SC., Ch. 3, 1 DC. in each of the next 2 SC., 2 DC. in each of the next 2 SC., 1 DC. in each of the next 3 SC., repeat from * around row, ending Ch. 3, 1 DC. in next SC., Ch. 10, 1 slip st. in 3rd Ch. of Ch. 5.

Row 5: Ch. 6, skip 2 Ch. and 1 DC., * 1 DC. in each of 7 DC., Ch. 3, skip 1 DC. and 3 Ch., 1 DC. in next DC., Ch. 3, skip 2 Ch., 1 DC. in next Ch., Ch. 2, skip 1 Ch., 1 DC. in next Ch., Ch. 2, 1 DC. in next Ch., Ch. 2, skip 1 Ch., 1 DC. in next Ch., Ch. 3, skip 2 Ch., ** 1 DC. in next DC., Ch. 3, skip 3 Ch. and 1 DC., repeat from * 2 times, then from * to ** ending row with 1 slip st. in 3rd Ch. of Ch. 6.

Row 6: Ch. 7, skip 3 Ch. and 1 DC., * 1 DC. in each of 5 DC., Ch. 4, skip 1 DC. and 3 Ch., 1 DC. in next DC., Ch. 3, skip 3 Ch., 1 DC. in next DC., Ch. 3, skip 2 Ch., 1 DC. in next DC., Ch. 2, 1 DC. in space, Ch. 2, 1 DC. in DC., Ch. 3, skip 2 Ch., 1 DC. in DC, Ch. 3, skip 3 Ch., ** 1 DC. in DC., Ch. 4, skip 3 Ch. and 1 DC., repeat from * 2 times, then from * to **, ending row with 1 slip st. in 3rd Ch. of Ch. 7.

Row 7: Ch. 7, skip 4 Ch. and 1 DC., 1 DC. in each of 3 DC., * Ch. 4, skip 1 DC. and 4 Ch., 1 DC. in next DC., Ch. 4, skip 3 Ch., 1 DC. in next DC., Ch. 4, skip 3 Ch., 1 DC. in next DC., Ch. 3, skip 1 Ch., 1 DC. in next Ch., 1 DC. in DC, 1 DC. in next Ch., Ch. 3, skip 1 Ch., 1 DC. in DC., Ch. 4, skip 3 Ch., 1 DC. in DC., Ch. 4, skip 3 Ch., 1 DC. in DC., ** Ch. 4, skip 4 Ch. and 1 DC., 1 DC. in each of 3 DC., repeat from * 2 times, then from * to ** ending row with Ch. 3, 1 slip st. in 3rd Ch. of Ch. 7.

Row 8: Ch. 4, skip 4 Ch. and 1 DC, 1 DC. in next DC., Ch. 4, 1 DC. in same DC., Ch. 3, skip 1 DC. and 4 Ch., 1 SC. in next DC. (1 pattern), * Ch. 3, skip 4 Ch., 1 DC. in next DC., Ch. 4, 1 DC. in same DC., Ch. 3, skip 4 Ch., 1 SC. in next DC. (pattern), Ch. 3, skip 3 Ch., 1 DC. in DC., 1 DC. in same DC., 1 DC. in next DC., Ch. 4, 1 DC. in same DC., 2 DC. in next DC., Ch. 3, skip 3 Ch., 1 SC. in next DC. (corner pattern), Ch. 3, skip 4 Ch., 1 DC. in next DC., Ch. 4, 1 DC. in same DC., ** Ch. 3, skip 4 Ch., 1 SC. in next DC. (pattern), Ch. 3, skip 4 Ch. and 1 DC., 1 DC. in next DC, Ch. 4, 1 DC. in same DC., Ch. 3, skip 1 DC. and 4 Ch., 1 SC. in next DC. (pattern), repeat from * then from * to ** ending row with Ch. 3, 1 slip st. in first Ch. of Ch. 4. Break thread.

There will be 3 patterns on each side and one corner pattern in each of the 4 corners.

To join motifs: When working last row of second motif, work as far as the first corner pattern, then * Ch. 3, skip 3 Ch., 1 DC. in next DC., Ch. 2, drop loop from hook, insert hook through corresponding pattern of first square and draw loop through, Ch. 2, 1 DC. in same DC., Ch. 3, skip 3 Ch., 1 SC. in next DC., repeat from * joining the 3 side patterns of the second motif to the corresponding 3 side patterns of the first motif. Join all motifs in this manner leaving the corner patterns free.

When 4 squares are joined, work the center figure as follows: Ch. 4, join in a ring, 3 SC. in ring, * Ch. 1, drop loop from hook, insert hook in space of first corner pattern, draw loop through, Ch. 1, 3 SC. in ring, repeat from * for each corner loop, ending with Ch. 1, 1 slip st. in first SC. Break thread.

Make 450 motifs for entire bedspread.

Bedspread of Filet

Bedspread of Filet

Original Materials - Crochet Cotton, 17 cones (800 yds.) White or Ecru.

Suggested Materials - Crochet Thread Size 10 or 12 or size of your choice – Optional - Use a Crochet Cotton if Preferred for a heavier bedspread

Crochet Hook Size 8.

Ch 1029, 1 tr in 9th ch from hook, 1 tr in every 3rd ch to end of row (341 meshes across spread or 13 patterns), ch 6 to turn and work 3 rows open meshes, then follow chart for desired length. (NOTE: There should be 3 open meshes on each side of finished patterns on spread in order to have a balanced-design for joining border.)

Work 1 row s c around spread as foundation to join border.

BORDER: Ch 39, 1 tr in 9th ch from hook (11 open meshes), ch 6 to turn and follow chart working border desired length.

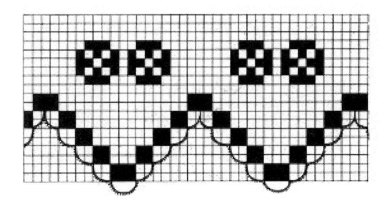

Join to spread with sc or by sewing.

Use Crochet Cotton, working stitch, to stitch and increasing at corner so that work lies flat. Join.

To Increase: Ch 11, 1 tr in 5th ch from hook, 1 tr in next 5 sts, tr over tr.

To Decrease: Sl st back.

EDGING:

Round 1: * Ch 11, sl st into corner of border, and repeat from * around joining at each corner.

Round 2: * Ch 5, sl st in first st of ch (picot), 1 sc over ch and repeat from * forming 4 picots over each ch, 11 with exception of point in which 5 picots are worked.

NOTE: Spread may be worked in strips and joined. When this is preferred, carry 2 open meshes each side of pattern design. When joined there will be 4 open meshes between patterns instead of 3 open meshes as given on chart.

Stafford Bedspread

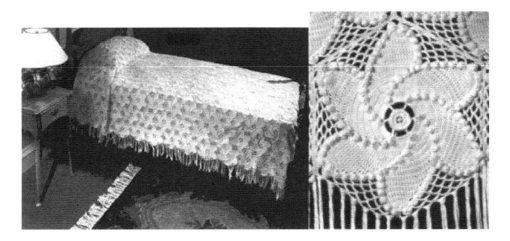

Stafford Bedspread

1 No. 9 Steel Crochet Hook

Scale: Each Hexagon about 6 1/4 inches wide

Original Materials MELLOSHEEN White or Ecru

This amount is sufficient for a single size spread.

The bedspread is approximately 58" x 88".

Suggested Materials - Crochet Thread Size 10 or 12 or size of your choice – Optional - Use a Crochet Cotton if Preferred for a heavier bedspread

MOTIF: (The popcorns are worked around each section after the motif is completed.)

Ch. 10, join in a ring.

Row 1: Ch. 3, 29 DC in ring, join.

Row 2: Ch. 13, * skip 4 DC, 1 DC in 5th DC, Ch. 10, repeat from * 5 times around, ending 1 slip st. in 3rd Ch. at start (6 loops).

Row 3: Ch. 3, 8 DC in first loop, * Ch. 4, 9 DC in next loop, repeat from * around, ending Ch. 4, slip st. in 3rd Ch. at start.

Row 4: Ch. 3, 1 DC in each of 6 DC, * Ch. 4, 4 DC in next space, 1 DC in each of 7 DC, repeat from * around, ending Ch. 4, 4 DC in last space, slip st. to 3rd Ch. at start.

Row 5: Ch. 3, 1 DC in each of 4 DC, * Ch. 4, 4 DC in space, 1 DC in each of 9 DC, repeat from * around, ending Ch. 4, 4 DC in space, 1 DC in each of 4 DC, slip st. to 3rd Ch. at start.

Row 6: Ch. 3, 1 DC in each of 2 DC, * Ch. 4, 4 DC in space, 1 DC in each of 11 DC, repeat from * around, ending Ch. 4, 4 DC. in space, 1 DC in each of 8 DC, slip st. to 3rd Ch. at start.

Row 7: Ch. 7, * 4 DC in space, 1 DC in each of 13 DC, Ch. 4, repeat from * around, ending 1 DC in each of 12 DC, slip st. to 3rd Ch. at start.

Row 8: Ch. 3, 3 DC in space, * 1 DC in each of 15 DC, Ch. 4, 4 DC in next space, repeat from * around, ending 1 DC in each of 15 DC, Ch. 4, slip st. to 3rd Ch. at start.

Row 9: Ch. 3, 1 DC in each of 16 DC, * Ch. 4, 1 SC in space, Ch. 4, 1 DC in each of 17 DC, repeat from * around, ending Ch. 4, 1 SC in space, Ch. 4, slip st. to 3rd Ch. at start (2 mesh between DC).

Row 10: Ch. 3, 1 DC in each of 14 DC, * Ch. 5, 1 SC in next mesh, Ch. 5, 1 SC in next mesh, Ch. 5, 1 DC in each of 15 DC, repeat from * around, ending Ch. 5, 1 SC in next mesh, Ch. 5, 1 SC in next mesh, Ch. 5, slip st. to 3rd Ch. at start (3 mesh between D. C).

Row 11: Ch. 3, 1 DC in each of 12 DC, * (Ch. 5, 1 SC in next mesh) 3 times, then Ch. 5, 1 DC in each of 13 DC, repeat from * around, ending (Ch. 5, 1 SC in next mesh) 3 times, Ch. 5, slip st. to 3rd Ch. at start (4 mesh between DC).

Row 12: Ch. 3, 1 DC in each of 10 DC, * Ch. 5, 1 SC in next mesh, (Ch. 6, 1 SC in next mesh) 3 times, Ch. 5, 1 DC in each of 11 DC, repeat from * around, ending after 3rd mesh, Ch. 5, slip st. to 3rd Ch. at start.

Row 13: Ch. 3, 1 DC in each of 8 DC, * Ch. 5, 1 SC in next mesh, (Ch. 6, 1 SC in next mesh) 4 times, Ch. 5, 1 DC in each of 9 DC, repeat from * around, ending after 5th mesh, Ch. 5, slip st. to 3rd Ch. at start.

Row 14: Ch. 3, then close the point as follows: * thread over, insert hook in next St., thread over and through st., thread over and through 2 loops only, leaving 2 loops on hook, repeat from * in each DC, always having one more loop on hook until there are 9 loops on hook, then thread over and through all loops on hook, Ch. 1 to tighten, Ch. 5, 1 SC in next mesh, (Ch. 7, 1 SC in next mesh) 5 times, Ch. 5, repeat from * around (having 10 loops on hook in each of the remaining 5 points), ending after 6th mesh, Ch. 5, 1 SC in center of first point, slip st. to center of first mesh.

Row 15: * Ch. 7, 1 SC in next mesh, repeat from * around, ending Ch. 7, 1 slip st. in slip st. at start of row.

Popcorn edge-Attach thread on first DC of Row 3 in any of the 6 sections, Ch. 3, 4 DC around same DC, slip hook out of last Ch. and insert in 3rd Ch. at start, draw dropped Ch. through to tighten (popcorn), * Ch. 1, 1 SC on the Ch. before 1st DC of Row 4 (in same section), then work 5 DC (popcorn) as before, repeat from * in each row to top of section and half way down the other side to end of mesh, working a popcorn in each mesh around point (19 popcorns). Repeat in each of the remaining 5 sections.

Center-Work 1 SC in front loop of each of the 30 DC around. Break thread.

Spider at Center-With darning needle and a strand of thread, weave spider at center as illustrated.

Make 149 motifs for entire bedspread.

Sew motifs together on wrong side as illustrated. Working back and forth, fill in upper edge with the Ch. mesh same as around motif.

Using four 9 inch strands of thread, knot fringe around both sides and lower edge.

Vine Square Bedspread and Pillow

Vine Square Bedspread and Pillow

DIRECTIONS

Original Materials Use 42 balls of Knitting & Crochet Cotton or 30 balls of Royal Society Cordichet Size 10.

Suggested Materials - Crochet Thread Size 10 or 12 or size of your choice – Optional - Use a Crochet Cotton if Preferred for a heavier bedspread

Size 9 Crochet Hook

Five squares across and six down with border on three sides will make a spread 90" x 112".

Square: Start at center square, ch 12, sl st in 1st ch.

1st row: Ch 3, 3 dc in ring, * ch 4 (corner), 4 dc in same ring, repeat from * 2 times, ch 4 (corner), sl st in 3rd ch.

2nd row: Ch 3, 1 dc in next 3 sts, * 3 dc in corner mesh, ch 4, 3 dc in same mesh, 1 dc in next 4 dc, repeat from *. Continue rows following diagram for pattern, always making 4 ch for corner mesh.

For Border: To increase on edge: Turn, ch 11, 1 dc in 9th ch from hook, 1 dc next 2 ch, 1 dc in last dc of row below.

To decrease on edge: Turn, ch 5, sk 3 dc, 1 dc in next dc, work across.

Vespers Bedspread

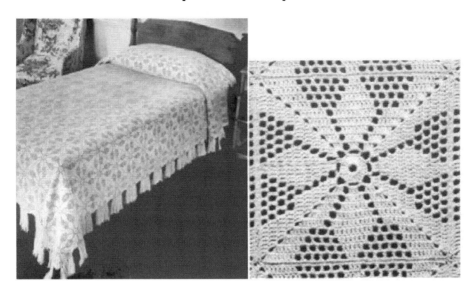

Vespers Bedspread

Original Materials : Coats Bedspread Cotton, 24 balls of White, or 19 balls of Ecru for double size spread; 19 balls of White, or 15 balls of Ecru for single size spread.

Stteel crochet hook No. 7 or 8.

Suggested Materials - Crochet Thread Size 10 or 12 or size of your choice – Optional - Use a Crochet Cotton if Preferred for a heavier bedspread

GAUGE: Each block measures about 5 inches square.

For a double size spread, 92 x 107 inches including fringe, make 17 x 20 blocks. For a single size spread, 72 x 107 inches including fringe, make 13 x 20 blocks.

BLOCK... Starting at center, ch 8, join with sl st to form ring.

1st rnd: Ch 3, 23 dc in ring. Join with sl st in 3rd st of ch-3 first made.

2nd rnd: Sc in same place as sl st, * ch 5, skip 2 dc, sc in next dc. Repeat from * around. Join last ch-5 with sl st to first sc made.

3rd rnd: Sl st in next loop, ch 3, 2 dc in same loop, * ch 2; in next loop make 3 dc, ch 2, 3 dc (corner); ch 2, 3 dc in next ch-5 loop. Repeat from * around, ending with ch 2. Join with sl st to 3rd st of ch-3 first made.

4th rnd: Ch 3, dc in each of next 2 dc, dc in ch-2 sp, ch 2, * skip 1 dc, dc in each of next 2 dc, 2 dc in ch-2 sp, ch 2, 2 dc in same sp (corner), dc in each of next 2 dc, ch 2, dc in next ch-2 sp, dc in each of next 3 dc, dc in ch-2 sp, ch 2. Repeat from * around, ending with dc in ch-2 sp. Join with sl st to 3rd st of ch-3 first made.

5th rnd: Ch 3, dc in each of next 3 dc, dc in ch-2 sp, ch 2, * skip 1 dc, dc in each of next 3 dc; in corner ch-2 make 2 dc, ch 2, 2 dc; dc in each of next 3 dc, ch 2, dc in ch-2 sp, dc in each of next 5 dc, dc in next ch-2 sp, ch 2. Repeat from * around, ending with dc in ch-2 sp, dc in last dc. Join.

6th rnd: Ch 3, dc in each of 4 dc, dc in ch-2 sp, ch 2, * skip 1 dc, dc in each of next 4 dc; in corner ch-2 make 2 dc, ch-2, 2 dc; dc in each of next 4 dc, ch 2, dc in next ch-2 sp, dc in each of next 7 dc, dc in ch-2 sp, ch 2. Repeat from * around, ending with dc in ch-2 sp, dc in each of last 2 dc. Join.

7th rnd: Ch 3, dc in each of next 5 dc, dc in ch-2 sp, ch 2, * skip 1 dc, dc in each of next 5 dc; in corner ch-2 make 2 dc, ch 2, 2 dc; dc in each of next 5 dc, ch 2, dc in next ch-2 sp, dc in each of next 9 dc, dc in ch-2 sp, ch 2. Repeat from * around, ending with dc in ch-2 sp, dc in each of last 3 dc. Join.

8th rnd: Ch 3, dc in each of next 5 dc, ch 2, * dc in next ch-2 sp, ch 2, skip 1 dc, dc in next dc, ch 2, skip 2 dc, dc in each of next 3 dc; in corner ch-2 make 2 dc, ch 2, 2 dc; dc in each of next 3 dc, ch 2, skip 2 dc, dc in next dc, ch 2, skip 1 dc, dc in next ch-2 sp, ch 2, skip 1 dc, dc in each of next 9 dc, ch 2. Repeat from * around, ending with 3 dc. Join.

9th rnd: Ch 3, dc in each of next 4 dc, ** ch 2, * dc in next sp, ch 2. Repeat from * 2 more times (3 sps), skip 1 dc, dc in each of next 4 dc; in corner ch-2 make 2 dc, ch 2, 2 dc; dc in each of next 4 dc, 3 sps, ch 2, skip 1 dc, dc in each of next 7 dc. Repeat from ** around, ending with 2 dc. Join.

10th rnd: Ch 3, dc in each of next 3 dc, * 4 sps, ch 2, skip 1 dc, dc in each of next 5 dc; in corner sp make 2 dc, ch 2, 2 dc; dc in each of next 5 dc, 4 sps, ch 2, skip 1 dc, dc in each of next 5 dc. Repeat from * around, ending with 1 dc. Join.

11th rnd: Ch 3, dc in each of next 2 dc, * 5 sps, ch 2, skip 1 dc, dc in each of next 6 dc; in corner sp make 2 dc, ch 2, 2 dc; dc in each of next 6 dc, 5 sps, ch 2, skip 1 dc, dc in each of next 3 dc. Repeat from * around, ending with 5 sps. Join last ch-2 to 3rd st of ch-3 first made. Fasten and break off. This completes one block.

Make necessary number of blocks, and sew together on wrong side with neat over-and-over stitches.

FRINGE...* Cut 10 strands, each 8 inches long. Double these strands, forming a loop. Pull loop through first sp, and draw loose ends through loop. Pull tight. Skip 1 sp. Repeat from * 3 more times, skip 1 sp, make a fringe in center of dc-block, skip 1 sp, and continue to make a fringe in every other sp across. Continue in this manner all around edges.

Cross Roads Bedspread

Cross Roads Bedspread

Original Materials: Crochet and Knitting Cotton, for double spread, 7 x 8 blocks (finished size about 92 x 106 inches) 28 skeins of White or Ecru; for single spread, 5 x 8 blocks (finished size about 66 x 106 inches) 20 skeins.

Steel crochet hook No. 4.

Suggested Materials – Crochet Cotton or Crochet Thread Size 10 or 12 or size of your choice – Optional - Use a Crochet Cotton if Preferred for a heavier bedspread

Gauge: Blocks are 13 1/4 inches square. (Each block requires about 400 yds. White or Ecru.)

Note: In the following directions, a sp refers to 1 dc, ch 1, 1 dc (instead of 1 dc, ch 2, 1 dc) and in making a bl, 1 dc is substituted for the ch-1.

Ch 35, turn.

1st row: 1 dc, in 7th ch from hook, ch 1, * skip 1 ch, 1 dc in next ch and repeat from * for length of foundation ch (15 sps). Ch 5, turn.

2nd row: Skip ch-1, 1 dc in next dc, * 1 dc in sp, 1 dc in next dc, and repeat from * 12 more times (27 dc). Ch 2, 1 dc in 3rd ch of turning ch-5. Ch 5, turn.

3rd row: Skip ch-2, 1 dc in each of next 3 dc (1 bl), * ch 1, skip 1 dc, 1 dc in next, and repeat from * 10 more times, making 11 sps, 1 dc in each of next 2 dc (1 bl), ch 2, 1 dc in 3rd ch, ch 5, turn.

4th row: Make bl over bl, 4 sps, then ch 1, skip 1 sp, 3 dc in next sp, ch 1, skip next ch-1, 1 dc in next dc, make 4 sps, 1 bl, ch 2, 1 dc in 3rd ch below, ch 5, turn.

5th row: Bl over bl, make 4 sps, 2 dc in next sp, ch 7, skip 3 dc, 2 dc in next sp, 1 dc in next dc, make 4 sps, 1 bl, ch 2, 1 dc in 3rd ch below, ch 5, turn.

6th row: Bl over bl, 3 sps, 2 dc in next sp, ch 4, 1 sc over ch 7, ch 4, skip 3 dc, 2 dc in sp, 1 dc in next dc, 3 sps, 1 bl, ch 2, 1 dc in 3rd ch below, ch 5, turn.

7th row: Bl over bl, 2 sps, 2 dc in next sp, ch 5, 1 sc over ch, 1 sc in sc, 1 sc over ch next to sc, make ch 5, skip 3 dc, 2 dc in next sp, 1 dc in next dc, 2 sps, bl over bl, ch 2, 1 dc in 3rd ch below. Ch 5, turn.

8th row: Bl over bl, 1 sp, 2 dc in next sp, ch 6, 1 sc over ch, 1 sc in each of 3 sc, 1 sc over ch, ch 6, skip 3 dc, 2 dc in sp, 1 dc in next dc, make 1 sp, bl over bl, ch 2, 1 dc in 3rd ch below, ch 5, turn.

9th row: Bl over bl, make 2 sps, 2 dc over ch, ch 6, skip 1st sc, put 1 sc in each of 2nd, 3rd and 4th sc's, ch 6, 2 dc over ch, 1 dc in 1st dc, make 2 sps, bl over bl, ch 2, 1 dc in 3rd ch below, ch 5, turn.

10th row: Bl over bl, make 3 sps, 2 dc over ch-5, ch 5, 1 sc in center sc of 3-sc group, ch 5, 2 dc over ch, 1 dc in 1st dc, make 3 sps, bl over bl, ch 2, 1 dc in 3rd ch below, ch 5, turn.

11th row: Bl over bl, make 4 sps, 2 dc over ch, ch 1, 2 dc over next ch, 1 dc in 1st dc, 4 sps, 1 bl, ch 2, 1 dc in 3rd ch below, ch 5, turn.

12th row: Bl over bl, 4 sps, ch 1, 3 dc in sp between 2 bls, 5 sps, 1 bl, ch 2, 1 dc in 3rd ch of row below, ch 5, turn.

13th row: 1 bl, 11 sps, 1 bl, ch 2, 1 dc in 3rd ch below, ch 5, turn.

14th row: 13 bls (27 dc), ch2, 1 dc in 3rd ch below, ch 5, turn.

15th row: Sp over sp, 13 more sps, ch 2, 1 dc in 3rd ch below. This finishes the center square. From this point the work is done around the 4 sides of the square and not back and forth. Ch 3, turn.

1st row: 2 dc in corner sp, then, working along the side of the center * make 13 bls, 3 dc in corner sp, ch 3, 3 more dc in same corner sp, and repeat from * around other 3 sides, ending row with ch 3, sl st to 3rd ch of ch-3 at beginning of row.

2nd row: Ch 3, 1 dc in each of next 3 dc, * 13 sps, dc in each of next 3 dc, 2 dc in corner sp, ch 3, 2 dc in same corner sp, dc in each of next 4 dc and repeat from * around. End this and all the following rows with sl st to ch-3 at beginning of row.

3rd row: Ch 3, 1 dc in each of next 3 dc, * 5 sps, ch 1, skip 1 sp, 3 dc in next sp, make 6 sps, dc in each of next 5 dc, 2 dc in corner sp, ch 3, 2 dc in same corner sp, dc in each of next 6 dc, and repeat from * around.

4th row: Ch 3, dc in each of next 3 dc. * 5 sps. 2 dc in next sp, ch 7, skip 3 dc, 2 dc fn next sp, 1 dc in next dc, 5 sps, dc in each of next 7 dc, 2 dc in corner sp, ch 3, 2 dc in same corner sp, dc in each of next 8 dc and repeat from * around.

5th row: Ch 3, dc in each of next 3 dc. * 4 sps, 2 dc in next sp, ch 4, 1 sc over ch-7, ch 4, skip 3 dc, 2 dc in next sp, 1 dc in next dc, 4 sps, dc in each of next 9 dc, 2 dc in corner sp, ch 3, 2 dc in same place, dc in each of next 10 dc and repeat from * around.

6th row: Ch 3, dc in each of next 3 dc, * 3 sps, 2 dc in next sp, ch 5, 1 sc over ch-4, 1 sc in sc, 1 sc over next ch, make ch 5, skip 3 dc, 2 dc in next sp, 1 dc in next dc, 3 sps, dc in each of next 11 dc, 2 dc in corner sp, ch 3, 2 dc in same place, dc in each of next 12 dc and repeat from * around.

7th row: Ch 3rd ch in each of next 3 dc, * 2 sps, 2 dc in next sp, ch 6, 1 sc over ch, 1 sc in each of next 3 sc, 1 sc over next ch, ch 6, 2 dc in next sp, 1 dc in next dc, 2 sps, dc in each of next 13 dc, 2 dc in corner sp, ch 3, 2 dc in same place, dc in each of next 14 dc, and repeat from * around.

8th row: Ch 3, dc in each of next 3 dc, * 3 sps, 2 dc over ch, ch 6, 1 sc in 2nd, 3rd and 4th sc's, ch 6, 2 dc over ch, 1 dc in 1st dc, 3 sps, dc in each dc of group, 2 dc in corner, ch 3, 2 dc in same place, dc in each dc of group and repeat from * around.

9th row: Ch 3, dc in each of next 3 dc, * 4 sps, 2 dc over ch, ch 5, 1 sc in center sc, ch 5, 2 dc over ch, 1 dc in 1st dc, 4 sps, dc in each dc of group, 2 dc in corner, ch 3, 2 dc in same place, dc in each dc of group and repeat from * around.

10th row: Ch 3, dc in each of next 3 dc. * 5 sps, 2 dc over ch-5, ch 1, 2 dc over next ch-5, 1 dc in 1st dc, 5 sps, dc in each dc of group, 2 dc in corner, ch 3, 2 dc in same corner, dc in each dc of group and repeat from * around.

11th row: Ch 3, dc in each of next 3 dc, * 5 sps, ch 1, skip 1 sp, 3 dc in next, 6 sps, dc in dc, ch 3, 2 dc in corner, dc in dc and repeat from * around.

12th row: Ch 3, dc in each of next 3 dc, * 13 sps, dc in each dc of group, 2 dc in corner, ch 3, 2 dc in same corner, dc in each dc of group and repeat from * around. Sl st to ch-3 at beginning of row, then sl st in each of next 3 dc.

13th row: Ch 3, * make 1 hi over each sp of row below, (13 bls), 12 sps, ch 1, 2 dc in corner, ch 3, 2 dc in same corner. 13 sps and repeat from * around. At the end of the row, ch 1, sl st to ch-3 at beginning-of row which completes the last sp.

14th to 22nd rows incl: Work around and around, making dc in each dc group (solid blocks), working medallion over each of the 13 sps, and increasing at corners as before. See illustration.

23rd row: Work a row of sps along the 4 sides, with 2 dc, ch 3, 2 dc in each corner.

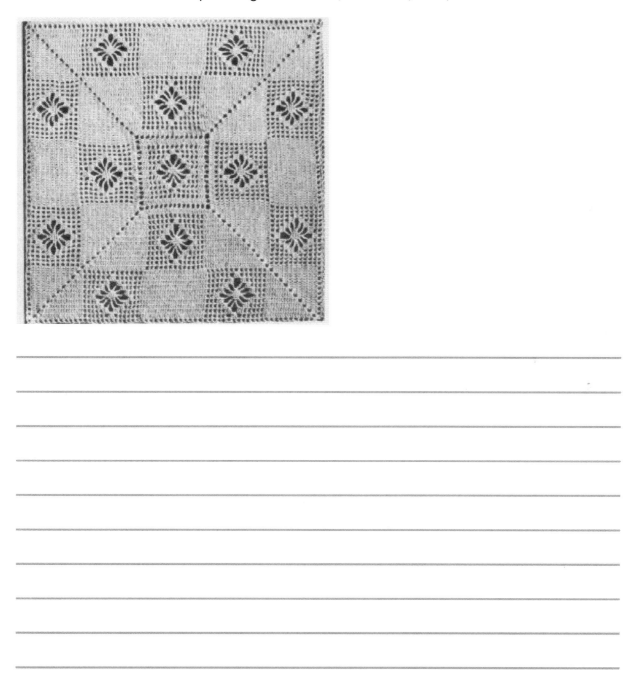

Royal Irish Rose Bedspread

Royal Irish Rose Bedspread

Original Materials - Mercerized Knitting & Crochet Cotton Royal Society   Eversheen Knitting & Crochet Cotton

62 balls for double bed	34 hanks
for double bed	
56 balls for single bed	31 hanks
for single bed	

Steel Crochet Hook No. 7 or 8

Suggested Materials – Crochet Cotton or Crochet Thread Size 10 or 12 or size of your choice – Optional - Use a Crochet Cotton if Preferred for a heavier bedspread

Rose: Ch 61, sl st in 1st ch to form ring.

1st rnd: Ch 6 (to count as 1 dc and ch-3), 1 dc in ring, * ch 3, 1 dc in ring, repeat from * twice, ch 3, sl st in 3rd ch of first ch-6 (5 sps).

2nd rnd: Ch 1, * in each sp make: 1 sc, 5 dc, 1 sc. Join with sl st to 1st sc.

3rd rnd: * Ch 5, sc in the st between the 2 petals, keeping ch-5 in back of petal, repeat from * 4 more times.

4th rnd: Ch 1. In each ch-5 loop make: 1 sc, 8 dc, 1 sc. Join with sl st in 1st sc.

5th rnd: Same as 3rd rnd, making ch-7's instead of ch-5's.

6th rnd: Ch 1. In each ch-7 loop make: 1 sc, 2 dc, 8 tr, 2 dc, 1 sc. Join with sl st to 1st sc.

Fasten off. Work another rose the same way, but at center of last petal of 2nd rose, ch 1, drop loop, insert hook in center of any petal of 1st rose, pull through dropped loop, ch 1, sl st into last tr, finish other half of petal. Fasten off.

Center Leaf: Ch 14.

1st row: 1 sc in 2nd ch from hook, 1 sc in each ch, (13 sc), ch 3, 1 sc in same ch as last sc, then make 10 more sc down the other side of foundation ch, turn.

2nd to 8th rows: ch 2, 1 sc in each sc (use back thread only), in next ch-3 make 2 sc with ch-3 between, then 1 sc in each sc down other side to with-in 3 sc from end, turn.

9th row: ch 2, 1 sc in each sc, 2 sc with ch-3 between in next ch-3. Fasten off.

2nd Leaf: repeat directions for center leaf, but at beginning of 9th row, ch 1, drop loop, insert hook in beginning of 9th row of 1st leaf, pull through dropped loop, and repeat 9th row.

3rd Leaf: Repeat directions for 2nd leaf, but join at opposite point on center leaf. Fasten off.

To Join Leaves to Rose: Attach thread in ch-3 of center leaf, ch 4, 1 sc in ch-3 of next leaf, ch 5, pick up roses, sl st in between 2 petals of one rose directly opposite the joined petal, 1 sc in each next 5 ch, sl st in ch-3 of 3rd leaf, 1 sc in next sc, 1 sc in next 4 ch of center leaf. Fasten off neatly in back of leaf.

Make another set of leaves and join the same way for opposite side.

Filet Fill-in: With right side of work towards you, attach to last lower point of right hand top leaf.

1st row: Ch 2, dc in middle st of rose petal after stem, ch 5, 2 tr in st between this petal and the next one, ch 5, 2 sc in middle st of next petal, ch 10, 1 tr between next 2 petals retaining 2 loops on hook, 1 tr at joining st of roses retaining 3 loops on hook, 1 tr in st between next 2 petals of next rose working off last 4 loops at once, ch 10, 2 sc in middle sts of next petal, ch 5, 2 tr between next 2 petals, ch 5, 1 dc in middle st of next petal, 1 dc in 1st point of side leaf, ch 4, 1 dc at next point of same leaf, turn.

2nd row: 1 tr in dc at base of ch-4 just made, ch 5, sk ch-5 of previous row, 1 tr in each of next 2 tr, ch 5, 1 tr in each of next 2 sc, ch 5, 1 tr in 5th st of next ch-10 loop, then thread over twice, insert hook in same ch where last tr was made, draw out a loop insert hook in 6th ch of next ch-10, draw out a loop, then work off loops 2 at a time, ch 5, 1 tr in each of next 2 sc, ch 5, 1 tr in each of next 2 tr, ch 5, 2 tr in last dc, dc in next point of leaf, ch 4 (ch 4 count for 1 tr), tr in next point of same leaf, turn.

3rd row: Sk first tr of row below, 1 tr next tr, continue working ch 5 over ch-5 and 1 tr in each tr, end row with tr in next free point of side leaf, ch 4, dtr in next point of same leaf, turn.

4th row: Same as 3rd row, ending with 1 dtr in next free point of side leaf. Fasten off.

Fill in other side to correspond. Fasten off.

Now, with right side of work towards you, attach thread to leaf point directly across that in which the last dtr was just worked, ch 4, dc in next point, ch 7, make a dtr in next point retaining last 3 loops on hook, thread over twice, insert hook in next free point of center leaf and draw out a loop (6 loops on hook), work off 2 loops at a time, ch 7, dc in next point, ch 4, sl st to next point, fasten off. Fill in three other openings between leaves in same manner.

Finishing Row: Attach thread with a sc at end point of center leaf, ch 2, 1 sc in same point, now work a row of ch 2 sps around entire motif, that is ch 2, skip 2 sts, 1 dc in next st and points of side leaves, put 2 sc with ch 2 between, continue with ch 2 sps, having 11 sps on each short side and 21 sps on each long side. Now work I row of sc in each dc and 2 sc in each sp, and 3 sc in each ch 2. Fasten off.

Join motifs as shown in Photograph, sewing together evenly, for double bed alternating rows across of 17 and 16 motifs; for single bed alternating row across of 14 and 13 motifs; and 13 motifs in length 215 motifs for double bed and 194 motifs for single bed.

Vintage Crochet Bedspreads – 31 Vintage Bedspread patterns to crochet

Crochet Notes

Made in United States
Troutdale, OR
10/30/2024